SHORT CUTS

INTRODUCTIONS TO FILM STUDIES

OTHER TITLES IN THE SHORT CUTS SERIES

THE HORROR GENRE: FROM BEELZEBUB TO BLAIR WITCH
Paul Wells

THE STAR SYSTEM: HOLLYWOOD'S PRODUCTION OF POPULAR IDENTITIES
Paul McDonald

SCIENCE FICTION CINEMA: FROM OUTERSPACE TO CYBERSPACE
Geoff King and Tanya Krzywinska

EARLY SOVIET CINEMA: INNOVATION, IDEOLOGY AND PROPAGANDA
David Gillespie

READING HOLLYWOOD: SPACES AND MEANINGS IN AMERICAN FILM
Deborah Thomas

DISASTER MOVIES: THE CINEMA OF CATASTROPHE
Stephen Keane

THE WESTERN GENRE: FROM LORDSBURG TO BIG WHISKEY
John Saunders

PSYCHOANALYSIS AND CINEMA: THE PLAY OF SHADOWS
Vicky Lebeau

COSTUME AND CINEMA: DRESS CODES IN POPULAR FILM
Sarah Street

MISE-EN-SCÈNE: FILM STYLE AND INTERPRETATION
John Gibbs

NEW CHINESE CINEMA: CHALLENGING REPRESENTATIONS
Sheila Cornelius with Ian Haydn Smith

SCENARIO: THE CRAFT OF SCREENWRITING
Tudor Gates

ANIMATION: GENRE AND AUTHORSHIP
Paul Wells

WOMEN'S CINEMA: THE CONTESTED SCREEN
Alison Butler

BRITISH SOCIAL REALISM: FROM DOCUMENTARY TO BRIT-GRIT
Samantha Lay

FILM EDITING: THE ART OF THE EXPRESSIVE
Valerie Orpen

AVANT-GARDE FILM: FORMS, THEMES AND PASSIONS
Michael O'Pray

PRODUCTION DESIGN: ARCHITECTS OF THE SCREEN
Jane Barnwell

NEW GERMAN CINEMA: IMAGES OF A GENERATION
Julia Knight

EARLY CINEMA

FROM FACTORY GATE TO DREAM FACTORY

SIMON POPPLE & JOE KEMBER

WALLFLOWER

LONDON and NEW YORK

A Wallflower Paperback

First published in Great Britain in 2004 by
Wallflower Press
4th Floor, 26 Shacklewell Lane, London E8 2EZ
www.wallflowerpress.co.uk

A catalogue record for this book is available from the British Library

ISBN 1 903364 58 2

Book Design by Rob Bowden Design

Printed in Great Britain by Antony Rowe Ltd, Chippenham, Wiltshire

CONTENTS

ACKNOWLEDGMENTS

Simon: I would like to thank all my colleagues at the University of Teesside Media Section, my co-author and particularly my parents, Judith, and my new son Marcus.

Joe: I would like to thank Simon, Tricia, my parents and brother for all their support.

In addition, the authors would particularly like to thank Richard Brown and Vanessa Toulmin.

PREFACE

Between 1895 and 1914, cinema established itself as the leading form of visual culture among rapidly expanding global media. It emerged from a rich tradition of scientific, economic, entertainment and educational practices, and rapidly developed as a worldwide institution. This book addresses current key areas of research in relation to the study and contextualisation of early cinema between 1895 and 1914. Its bias is predominantly British, although American and European cinemas are considered. The text introduces undergraduate students to the study of cinema as a series of aesthetic, technological, cultural, ideological and economic debates. It explores new and traditional readings of early cinema, and is divided into distinct thematic sections which offer approaches to the subject which can be readily developed by students.

Chapter 1 provides an introductory overview to the key contextual and historic events in the development of cinema between 1895 and 1914, and introduces key thematic topics which are developed by subsequent chapters.

Chapter 2 considers the importance of studying early cinema and provides a survey of key academic approaches to the subject.

Chapter 3 deals with the uses to which the new medium was put and examines some of the key roles it played within new mass industrial societies. It looks at the role of cinema as a form of entertainment, education, indoctrination and escape, and offers some strategies for dealing with a wide range of early cinema and cinema related resources.

Chapter 4 approaches the issue of the roles of cinema from a different perspective, arguing that the exhibitors of early films played a vital role in their consumption. It also deals with the reception of early film, showing how the form of the films themselves impacted upon their first audiences.

Chapter 5 concludes the book with an analysis of the development of narrative style, genre and film form in the period 1895–1914.

We hope that this book will therefore serve as an appropriate introduction to the study of Early Cinema and aid in the development of research into this essential area of contemporary Film Studies.

Simon Popple & Joe Kember
January 2004

1 CINEMA 1895–1914

Such a bustle and a hurry
O'er the 'living picture' craze
Rivals rushing full of worry
In these advertising days.
Each the first and each the only
Each the others widely chaff
All of them proclaiming boldly
Their's the first A-Kind-O-Graph.
But its a wonder really
How the constant flood of life
O'er the screen keeps moving freely
Full of action – stir and strife.
There the waves are wildly breaking
There the swimmer stems the tide.
The cyclist his record making,
With the countless varied scenes beside.
'Tis far from perfect in its movements
'Tis very hard upon the eyes;
The jolty wobble no improvements,
Smooth running films a surprise.
Still successful beyond reason,
Spite of all its erring ways,
Holding first place in the season
Is the 'Living Picture' craze.
                    – *British Journal of Photography*, 4 December 1896

First Readings

The first reviews of early cinema performances reveal many of the issues which are still at the heart of our readings of cinema over a century later. They are full of promise, delight and wonder at the 'Living Picture craze'. The following early British review greets cinema as a welcome extension of photography and as the 'most perfect' means of representing reality. It describes a tendency to regard the technology of cinema as an objectified recorder of contemporary life, an adjunct of the 'scientifically rational' art of photography, with the added dimension of movement:

> Of all the marvels that have recently been brought to light in the way of photography the 'Cinématographe', which reproduces photographs of actual scenes and persons from life – moving, breathing, in fact, living pictures – is the most startling and sensational, if not the most original, as in the case of invisible photography. It is the most perfect illustration that has heretofore been attempted in photography. Without the aid of any of the usual paraphernalia of the photographer, pictures are thrown on a screen through the medium of the 'Cinématographe' with a realism that baffles description. (Anon. 1896)

This reaction is typical of the range of early enthusiastic reviews, but by no means the only response to cinema. Many commentators were concerned with technical imperfections in lighting, in image quality and in the fidelity of the moving image. Maxim Gorky, reviewing one of the first cinema shows in Russia, asked his readers to look beyond the initial thrill of the moving image and to consider its shortfalls, its lack of colour, dimension and real sound:

> Last night I was in the Kingdom of Shadows. If you only knew how strange it is to be there. It is a world without sound, without colour. Everything there – the earth, the trees, the people, the water and the air – is dipped in monotonous grey. Grey rays of the sun across the

sky, grey eyes in grey faces, and the leaves of the trees are ashen grey. It is not life but its shadow, it is not motion but its soundless spectre. Here I shall try to explain myself, lest I be suspected of madness or indulgence in symbolism. I was at Aumont's and saw Lumière's cinématograph – moving photography. The extraordinary impression is so unique and complex that I doubt my ability to describe it with all its nuances. (Gorky 1896)

Gorky exposes a series of contradictions at the heart of cinema. He sees it as both mesmeric and profoundly affecting, but at the same time a pale simulacrum of life. His reading, at such an early phase of cinema's development, prefigures the hope and pessimism with which we still regard the developing mass media in contemporary society. This sense of ambivalence and cynicism, which came to full fruition at the *fin-de-siècle*, was a response to the process of modernisation and industrialisation that had emerged in the West during the nineteenth century. Technological and cultural progress cast an intoxicating spell, as Gorky acknowledged, but it also triggered a disenchantment with certain aspects of modernity. This critique focused on the populist, market-led and low-cultural aspirations that he identified with the Lumière show:

I am convinced that these pictures will soon be replaced by others of a genre more suited to the general tone of the *Concert Parisien*. For example, they will show a picture entitled: *As She Undresses*, or *Madam at her Bath*, or *A Woman in Stockings*. They could also depict a sordid squabble between a husband and wife and serve it to the public under the heading of *The Blessings of Family Life*.

Yes, no doubt, this is how it will be done. The bucolic and the idyll could not possibly find their place in Russia's markets thirsting for the piquant and the extravagant. I also could suggest a few themes for development by means of a cinematograph and for the amusement of the marketplace. For instance: to impale a fashionable parasite upon a picket fence, as is the way of the Turks, photograph him, then show it. It is not exactly piquant but quite edifying.

The fin-de-siècle context

As Gorky recognised, the cinema emerged from a period of intense modernisation, in which the conditions of everyday life were subject to rapid and unprecedented change. During the nineteenth century the chiefly rural populations of the industrialising Western nations had poured into the cities as a response to the development of the factory and the increasing rationalisation of industrial labour. For example, by 1901 around 75 per cent of the British population lived in an urban setting – a situation repeated throughout Europe and the United States. As this vast metropolitan melée became more organised, the longstanding political power of landowning classes appeared to be on the wane, and the working-class labour movement became more influential. Although poverty remained widespread, the demand for universal welfare seemed an achievable ideal for many. Meanwhile, the middle class grew rapidly, a population accommodated within the new suburbs of large cities and connected by a diversifying transport and communications network. The motorcar, the electric tram, the motor bus and the passenger liner joined the train in revolutionising freedom of movement for the increasing numbers that could afford it. Modern transportation gave many the opportunity to accommodate an increasing amount of leisure time into a day otherwise spent in the workplace and at home – a development that resulted in the rapid expansion and diversification of sporting facilities and of escapist popular entertainments, such as the cinema. It also allowed the industrial development of domestic and international tourism, giving the urban middle classes a privileged, if rather distant and shallow, perspective on a wide range of other landscapes and cultures.

As individuals strove to accommodate new roles in the workplace and the leisure space, the question of personal identity came increasingly into question. In particular, as the female middle class, led initially by the suffrage movement, began to exploit new openings in the labour market, old certainties about the patriarchal structure of family life came under immense pressure. The clear identities of the male as breadwinner and female as housewife and child-rearer were subjected to intense scrutiny, leaving some to yearn for 'lost traditions' of domestic identity and others to grow impatient for legislation to initiate genuine change. The fight for universal suffrage thus exemplifies the confrontation – also uncovered in Gorky's review of the Cinématographe – between the weight of tradition and the seemingly unstoppable march of progress.

Thus, even a cursory glance at this remarkable period of historical development inevitably reveals that beneath the polished surface of increasingly rationalised, wealthy and technologically-dependent societies were a welter of anxieties concerning the nature and consequences of progress. These were powerfully registered in the increasingly fragmented nature of artistic endeavour from the turn of the century. Modernist writers, painters and musicians all began to experiment with new forms of representation and expression, seeking to challenge artistic traditions that no longer seemed adequate reflections of contemporary experience. Similarly, cinema underwent a remarkable period of invention and transition. Indeed, arguably it became the arena in which the pressures of modernity were most fully played out. However, unlike other artistic canons, which became more fragmented, eclectic and elitist, the cinema typifies the emergence of a new populist tradition that has dominated mass media culture throughout the twentieth century. From a small-scale and often artisanal enterprise, film production and exhibition grew exponentially in this period, reaching millions across continents, and branching across race, social, gender and age classifications. We now offer a brief chronology of this development, registering the central events in this consolidation of industrial, commercial, social and personal interests.

The development of the moving picture – a chronology

The institutional changes wrought between 1895 and 1914, and the roles performed by cinema around the turn of the century, were profound. For example, by 1914 the cinema in Britain had evolved from its original uncertain status as an entertainment novelty to a commercially important institution in its own right. Cinema had undergone a transition from its original home within the music hall and the travelling fairground shows, and had graduated from the small shop-front shows called 'Penny Gaffs' of the late Victorian and early Edwardian period, to the purpose-built picture palaces which had sprung up in most provincial towns by 1914. Fairground cinemas, where most ordinary people first experienced moving pictures, had all but disappeared, and the transitory nature of these performances became regularised and fixed to specific locations (see Toulmin 1994). At the same time a gradual transition took place from mixed entertainments, which included cinema amongst a myriad of competing and complementary attractions, to a new set of performance practices in which film was the sole or dominant element.

Going to the cinema had become a regular occupation for most strata of British society, although its clientele was still predominantly working class, and it was fast becoming the nation's main entertainment and information source. The industry itself, that is the film producing, distribution, and exhibition sectors of the business, had grown substantially in this period. The beginnings of integration across these three sectors began to develop with companies attempting to control as many aspects of the industry as possible. Not only did the nature of exhibition change during this period, but the style and form of films rapidly evolved, incorporating longer and more complex narratives.

What follows is a brief chronological survey of the key developments in the evolution of cinema between 1895 and 1914, which highlights major personalities, events, and technological and industrial break-throughs. The chronology is by no means exhaustive and is intended as an indicative resource. It provides a sense of the dynamic and complex international nature of early cinema. Its primary aim is to establish a linear historical framework within which the thematic approach to early cinema adopted by each chapter can be contextualised.

1895

The year which saw the launch of commercial cinema was dominated by the race to perfect an apparatus to capture and project moving photographic images for a mass audience. In America, Thomas Edison's

Kinetoscope, a type of peep-show device, launched commercially in 1893, had already become a prominent filmic presence in sideshows, penny gaffs and Kinetoscope parlours across the US and Europe. However, each machine could only serve an audience of one, and was limited to exhibiting a single short film. Edison's domination of the fledgling market was soon threatened by a host of competitors seeking to develop their own film-making and projection technologies. Yet it was in Europe that the major threat to Edison's monopoly emerged. In Britain the partnership of engineer Robert W. Paul and photographer and lanternist Birt Acres was forged to provide a means of making films for copies of Edison's Kinetoscope, which Paul had begun manufacturing. A camera was developed and several films were shot in the spring and summer. However, key to the development of cinema as we know it was the pioneering work of photographic manufacturers Auguste and Louis Lumière, who were pre-eminent in the early development of an apparatus for taking and exhibiting moving pictures. Their Cinématographe, from which cinema derives its name, was a combination of camera and projector. It was one of the most successfully exploited machines in the early period of commercial cinema, using a 35mm nitrate-based celluloid film.

The Cinématographe was patented on 13 February 1895, and on 19 March Louis Lumière made his first film, *La Sortie des usines Lumière*. Following a series of private screenings the Lumières presented their first public performance on 28 December 1895 in the 'Salon Indien' of the Grand Café in Paris to just 33 people. This inauspicious performance is widely regarded as the 'birth of public cinema'.

Technological advances

A host of pioneers were responsible for concurrent international developments of moving picture apparatus. Key figures included Eugène Lauste and Max Skladanowsky.

- Lauste produced the Panoptikon projector for the Latham Brothers in April, which was premiered in New York on 20 May.
- In Germany, Skladanowsky demonstrated his Bioskop projector at the Wintergarten in Berlin on 1 November.

Industry developments

The nascent film industry was an international phenomenon, and several important players emerged during this year in Britain, France, the US and Germany.

- In France, Léon Gaumont and Co. was founded on 12 August.
- In the US The American Mutoscope Company was founded in Jersey City on 27 December.

1896

Following the premiere of the Cinématographe in Paris, the Lumières began a rapid programme of exhibition across Europe and the US. They commissioned a series of agents to promote exhibitions and licensed cameramen to produce films from around the globe. The Cinématographe premiered in England on 25 January at the Regent Street Polytechnic, and in the US at Keith's Theater, New York, on 29 June. On 14 January Birt Acres gave his first demonstration of film projection at the Royal Photographic Society, shortly followed by his ex-business partner Robert Paul, who demonstrated the Theatograph at Finsbury Technical College on 20 February.

In the US Thomas Edison began his bid to control the industry and purchased the rights to Armat and Jenkins' Phantascope, re-named the Vitascope, which was premiered on 23 April at Koster & Bial's New York Music Hall. This was closely followed by the public premiere of the American Mutoscope Co's Biograph projector at the Hammerstein Theater, New York, on 12 October.

This projector used 68mm film, not 35mm, as employed by the majority of early film-makers. 35mm would become the industry standard, but most of these early film systems were incompatible because of either the size of the film gauge, or the size and spacing of film sprockets. The Lumière system relied on circular sprocket holes and was thus incompatible with Edison's square sprockets. This protected the copyright of film prints and allowed individuals to more fully control their films, but was a frustrating factor in terms of opening up the marketplace to competitors. Another early factor was the tendency to sell prints outright to potential exhibitors. This proved an expensive proposition because prints only had a limited commercial life. In the first ten years of cinema the tendency to rent films gradually replaced direct sales as the market widened and the technology of film projection became more and more standardised.

Edison's efforts would characterise attempts to control the technological development of cinema through patent law, and would include attempts to protect American markets at home and abroad, even to the extent of preventing European films being seen in the US.

Technological advances
- Auguste Blaise Baron began his experimentation with synchronised recorded sound.
- Edison and Paul independently exhibited the first hand-coloured films.

Industry developments
As cinema began to embed itself within existing entertainment attractions a growing market for projection and film apparatus developed. Pioneers' attempts to consolidate their market position by controlling the production and exhibition of films were rapidly eroded by the sale of apparatus and new production companies.
- Paul's Animatographe become commercially available, and new producers entered the market.
- The Pathé Frères Company was established in Paris on 1 November.

1897

This year was characterised by the beginnings of major production companies and the construction of purpose-built studios throughout Europe and the US. In the UK James Williamson and George Albert Smith began production of films on the south coast and Robert W. Paul founded The Paul Animatograph Company.

The lanternist and shoemaker William Slade commenced his cinematographic tour of the UK. This tour, which visited a range of non-metropolitan venues including town halls, fairs, music halls and even two Royal Navy warships, is indicative of the variety of contexts within which cinema performances took place and exemplifies the development of speculative regional ventures into the film trade.

In Paris the cinematograph fire at the Charity Bazaar of 4 May left 121 dead, and in London films of Queen Victoria's Golden Jubilee demonstrated the popularity of news events with film audiences. The first major book on cinema, Cecil Hepworth's *The ABC of the Cinematograph*, was published.

Technological advances

- Herman Casler's Mutoscope flip frame viewer was launched. It became commonly known as the 'What the Butler saw' due to its subsequent association with risqué subjects. The machine became a popular feature of leisure venues and middle-class homes.
- Henry W. Short's Filoscope flip book viewer was also marketed, featuring films made by Robert W. Paul.
- The Kinora, a handheld viewing device, was developed by Louis Lumière.
- Raoul Grimoin-Sanson patented the Cinécosmorama, a panoramic projection system.

Industry developments

- The magician and trick film-maker Georges Méliès opened his film studios at Montreuil-sous-Bois on 22 March, and established Star Films.
- In the same month Léon Gaumont started the production of film in Paris under the direction of Alice Guy.
- The Vitagraph company was founded in New York on 31 March by Stuart Blackton and Albert Smith.
- Pathé Frères began production in December, founding a new company, the General Company of Cinematographs, Phonographs and Film.
- The Lumière Cinématographe became commercially available.
- Thomas Edison continued legal attempts to control the film industry with a series of prosecutions in the courts under US patent law.
- Film copyrighting was instituted in Britain at the Stationer's Hall and the US at the Library of Congress.

1898

The first film manifesto was produced by Polish film-maker, Bolesław Matuszewski, entitled *Une Nouvelle Source d'Histoire*. He advanced the argument that film was a vital form of historical record and should be collected and preserved as such. One such historical event was the Spanish-American War which became a focus for early actuality footage. Many of the films produced were fake reconstructions of real and imagined events. For example, Georges Méliès produced *Visite Sous-marin du Maine* (*The Wreck of the Maine*) which depicted a visit to the wreck of the warship allegedly sunk in Cuba by the Spanish that had triggered the war.

Notions of celebrity were further established when Pope Leo XII was filmed by W. K. L. Dickson for the Biograph company, and religious controversy was triggered when the Pope gave a blessing direct to camera.

New uses for moving pictures were constantly heralded in the press of the period; one such application, the surgical film, was pioneered in Paris by Dr Eugène-Louis Doyen.

Technological advances

- In April, Auguste Baron patented a synchronised sound system.
- J. A. Prestwich marketed a film magazine which could hold up to 400ft of film, allowing the production of longer films.
- Oskar Messter launched the Amateur-Kinetograph, a combined amateur camera and projector using 35mm film.
- William Charles Hughes marketed the Hughes' Street Cinema-tograph, an enclosed portable device with multiple peepholes allowing customers on the street to view projected images.

Industry developments

- In London Charles Urban founded the Warwick Trading Company on behalf of the Edison company.
- A. C. Bromhead and T. A. Walsh launched the Gaumont Company, Britain.
- Charles Pathé opened new studios at Vincennes, France.
- Vitagraph began production of films in May and were licensed to

work for Edison from July following the resolution of legal action over patent rights.

1899

The two major attractions for film-makers and audiences were the resolution of the Dreyfuss affair in France and the outbreak of the Anglo-Boer War in South Africa. The Dreyfuss Affair centred on false allegations of spying within the French army. Alfred Dreyfuss, a Jewish-French officer, was convicted of spying for Germany on false evidence and exiled to Devil's Island. He was re-tried and subsequently pardoned in 1899, and the affair bitterly divided French society, unleashing waves of anti-semitism and inciting violent demonstrations. Film-makers such as Georges Méliès were quick to produce dramatised re-enactments of the case. A similar tendency to dramatise newsworthy events was demonstrated throughout the Boer war, as some film-makers attempted to satisfy the public demand for wartime scenes. Other cameramen, such as W. K. L. Dickson and Joe Rosenthal, produced series of genuine films from the front.

In the UK, the Bamforth Co., in association with Riley Brothers, further developed the regional film industry, as they began their first phase of major film production as an extension of their lantern slide business.

Technical advances
- Auguste Baron patented his Graphonoscope, a further advance in his experimentation with synchronised sound systems.
- F. M. Lee and E. R. Turner patented a three-colour film process in the UK.
- Birt Acres launched the Biokam, a combined amateur camera and projector which used 17.5mm film.

Industry developments
- In September, Robert W. Paul opened his own studios next to his Theatrograph and Animatograph Factory, in New Southgate, UK.

1900

At the Exposition Universale of 1900 in Paris, two attempts were made to improve upon the spectacle of moving pictures in terms of image size and scale. The Lumières attempted 75mm projection for the first time, but were forced to return to the usual 35mm format in order to project the image upon a 400 square metre canvas. Raoul Grimoin-Sanson's Cinéorama system of ten projectors was intended to produce 360º film projection, but proved inoperable due to severe fire risks. However, Léon Gaumont successfully demonstrated his new 'Chronophone' apparatus for synchronising image and sound at the *Exposition*, screening a full-sized image of himself speaking.

Among the primary attractions of the year was the continuing dominance of Boer War subjects, including celebrated fakes by James White in the US and the Mitchell and Kenyon Co. in the UK. The Boxer Rebellion also provided film-makers and audiences with fertile military subject matter, largely satisfied by reconstructions such as James Williamson's *Attack on a China Mission*, which was shot in the seaside town of Hove, UK.

Technological developments
- A range of amateur film cameras and projectors were launched, including the Pocket-Chrono – an amateur machine which could record and project film within the home.

Industry developments
- In the US, Edison terminated Vitagraph's licence due to a dispute over royalties.
- In Berlin, Oskar Messter established a film production company, Messter Projections.

1901

World events were dominated by the death of Queen Victoria and the assassination of President McKinley in the US. Queen Victoria's funeral was filmed by several prominent film companies and proved a major attraction across the world. Filming the event led to heated competition amongst film companies as they vied for the best vantage points along the route of the procession, and then rushed to develop, distribute and screen their films before any of their competitors. Indeed, the notion of instantaneous news coverage was firmly established by this event. In the US, the assassination of McKinley by Leon Czolgosz fired the public with curiosity. In response, the Edison Company produced *The Execution of Czolgosz*, a film including footage of the prison in which he was held followed by a dramatic re-enactment of his execution by electrocution.

Technological advances
- George Grivolas attempted three-dimensional film projection.

Industry developments
- Edison's legal battle with Vitagraph continued in the courts
- In France, Pathé increased their rate of film production.

1902

Léon Gaumont continued development of the Chronophone film sound system and successfully demonstrated it to the French photographic society in November. Gaumont's experiments were mirrored by many other, less commercially successful, attempts to successfully synchronise image and sound recordings. Also in France, Georges Méliès' productions became increasingly lavish, and his release of *Voyage dans la Lune* secured his position as premier producer of fantasy and trick films. The diversity of French film production in this year is evidenced by Eugène-Louis Doyen's gruesome and genuine film depicting the surgical separation of Siamese twins 'Doodica' and 'Radica'. The film sparked a short-lived international controversy and opened new debates concerning the dubious uses to which moving pictures were being put.

Industry developments
- Vitagraph won a landmark victory in the patents war against Edison and was able to begin the production of films once again.
- The Will Barker Co. began production at Ealing in London.

- The Electric Cinema, possibly the first purpose-built cinema, opened in Los Angeles.
- Charles Pathé set up his own studio at Vincennes and employed Ferdinand Zecca to head production of trick-oriented films in direct competition with George Méliès.
- Charles Urban resigned from the Warwick Trading Company to establish his own company, the Urban Trading Company

1903

In response to the copying of his films Georges Méliès opened an American branch of Star Films in New York, which was controlled by his son Gaston. The Urban Trading Company began a major production programme of topical, topographical and scientific films in the UK, including *the Unseen World* series, which presented to audiences magnified images of natural history subjects. In the US, Edison's chief cameraman, Edwin Stanford Porter, shot *The Great Train Robbery*, which is controversially regarded as the origin of the western film genre. As in many films of the period, this film borrowed substantially from earlier productions, particularly in its use of the chase scene and conventions of cross-cutting between action.

Industry developments
- Pathé opened their London branch.
- Gaumont established an English company, Gaumont Ltd, under the directorship of A. C. Bromhead.

1904

There was a marked expansion of the moving picture trade. This was especially evident in the US, where the number of purpose-built picture theatres rapidly increased. As part of this expansion, European firms, such as Pathé, began an aggressive assault on the US market. Pathé opened their own factory, retail outlet and studios dedicated to the tastes and preoccupations of American audiences. At the St. Louis Fair, Hales Tours, an attempt to use cinema as part of a virtual reality machine, was premiered. It would prove one of the most successful single attractions of the period.

Technological advances
- Lucien Bull pioneered high-speed cinematography filming the progress of a bullet using electro-flash cinematography.

Industry developments
- Charles Pathé built a new studio complex in Montreuil, France.
- Filoteo Albertini opened the first purpose built cinema in Italy, the Cinema Moderno, Rome.
- The Clarendon Film Co. opened elaborate studios in Croydon, UK.

1905

The first Nickelodeon opened in the US on 6 November. The name was the creation of John P. Harris and Harry Davis who used it to describe a shop-front cinema they were running in Pittsburgh which charged a nickel for admission. The name subsequently became synonymous with cinema in the US.

Max Linder made his first film appearance in a Pathé title, *A Schoolboy's First Day Out*. Linder quickly became one of the biggest early film stars, establishing his own identity as 'Max' from 1907 and helping to initiate the star system in cinema. He built his reputation as a loveable rogue and can be seen as major influence on Charlie Chaplin and other comic stars.

Technological advances
- Pathé launched the Pathécolor stencil system which mechanised the process of colouring film prints.
- The Pathé Professional Studio camera was introduced. It became the industry standard for many years and was used to shoot D. W. Griffith's landmark film, *Birth of a Nation* (1915).

Industry development
- In the UK, the famous Biograph Cinema opened in London.

1906

New processes of colour cinematography began to reach fruition. Early colour processes pioneered by Lee and Turner and William Friese-Greene provided the impetus for G. A. Smith and Charles Urban in the development of the Kinemacolor process, which was patented in this year. Scandinavian film-making was consolidated by the development of The Nordisk Film Company, founded in Denmark by Ole Olsen and Arnold Nielsen.

Technological advances
- Eugene Lauste patented a sound-on-film process, and Gaumont launched the Elgéphone amplifier for film-sound performances.

Industry developments
- The Daily Bioscope news cinema opened in London.
- A major film distribution company, the Western Film Exchange, was established in Chicago by Harry Aitken and John F. Freuler during July and was shortly followed by the Carl Laemmle Film Service in October.
- Charles Urban created a new company to replace the Urban Trading Company in France, the Société Générale des Cinématographes Eclipses.

1907

In the UK, *Kinematograph Weekly*, Britain's first trade journal dedicated purely to the film business, was founded. The journal provided a comprehensive guide to the film industry, a forum for debate about industrial developments and, crucially, reviews and advertisements for new equipment and film rentals. Many of these functions had been performed by non-specialist journals such as *The Era*, *The Showman* and *The World's Fair*. Trade magazines dedicated to the film industry increasingly developed in the US and Europe.

Britain's first purpose-built cinema, The Central Hall, in Colne, opened in February. It was built by Joshua Duckworth, whose previous profession was that of magic lantern showman.

Technological advances
- Cecil Hepworth developed the Vivaphone sound system.

1908

In the US, the actor D. W. Griffith was appointed by the Biograph Company to produce films, the first of which was *The Adventures of Dollie*. Griffith was to become a pre-eminent figure in the historical development of US film production, consolidating the storytelling capacity of the medium with stylish innovations in the editing of moving pictures. Meanwhile, Biograph's most important employee was Florence Lawrence, who was introduced to the world as 'The Biograph Girl', and whose face would adorn posters and advertisements, as well as cinema screens, throughout the world. Lawrence proved definitively to film companies that individual stars could be the most important factor in attracting audiences to the cinema. Another key innovation in this year was the launch of the film serial by Éclair Films in France, who adapted the popular series of novels featuring the detective Nick Carter. The serial was directed by Victorin Jasset, and brought an episodic storyline to audiences of moving pictures, an adaptation of the literary tradition of the serial publication of stories in periodicals.

Technological advances
- Kinemacolor was premiered at the Royal Society of Arts on 9 December.

Industry developments
- The US imposed a duty on foreign film imports in an attempt to protect their own market.
- The Gaumont Film Co. held their inaugural trade fair in London.
- The Berlin Convention clarified, for the first time in Europe, that legislation was needed for copyright provision on moving pictures.

1909

This year saw the first direct government legislation aimed at the regulation of the cinema industry in Britain. The Cinematograph Film Act was primarily an attempt to regulate the conditions within which film performances took place and protect a growing audience against the ever-present threat of fire. Cinematograph shows on travelling fairgrounds were excluded from the provisions of this Act, but for other showmen, working within small non-theatrical venues, such as the penny gaff, this was a serious blow, since they could not afford to conform to the stringent new regulations.

In the US, the Motion Picture Patents Company (MPPC) was formed by Edison, Vitagraph and Biograph in order to control the production of films. In effect no company outside the trust was legally entitled to buy film stock and thus produce pictures. Over 10,000 exhibitors signed an agreement to only show films produced by trust members. The International Congress of Film Producers' meeting in Paris attempted to establish a rival trust, under the encouragement of George Eastman, President of Kodak.

Industry developments
- A raft of new American production companies were launched, including Rex, Yankee, Powers Picture Plays, Bison and Carl Laemlle's Independent Motion Pictures Company of America (IMP). IMP was formed to challenge the MPPC.
- Vitagraph launched Florence Turner as the Vitagraph Girl in response to Biograph's success with the Biograph Girl.
- Mary Pickford, arguably the most famous star of the silent period, made her first film appearance in D. W. Griffith's *The Violin Maker of Cremona*.

1910

The longstanding fascination of film audiences for newsworthy events was now fully exploited by Pathé, who inaugurated weekly newsreels. Within the rapidly spreading picture theatres of the US and Europe, newsreel footage became a popular and conventional part of film programmes that might also include comedies, melodramas, serials and even advertisements.

Technological advances
- The Allfex sound effects machine was launched by A. H. Moorhouse to provide a vast array of effects to accompany cinema performances.

Industry developments
- Asta Nielsen made her first screen appearance in *The Abyss*; Nielsen became one of the most popular European stars.

1911

The length of films had been gradually increasing, from the initial single-scene, one-minute productions of the Lumières and their contemporaries, to multi-scene dramatic story films. For example, *The Tale of Two Cities*, issued by Vitagraph, at three reels and approximately 45 minutes, was indicative of the move towards feature films. By 1911, longer films were proving more and more attractive to exhibitors and audiences, and were usually at the top of the bill in cinemas. Due to their elevated position within the programme, they earned the name 'feature film' and were distinguished by their length – each was usually a minimum of three to four reels. However, silent films were shot and projected at different speeds. Many cameras and projectors were hand-cranked, with electrical mechanisms only gradually replacing this manual method. Most film projectors whether manual or electric were vari-speed so the length of performances could be varied, sometimes for dramatic effect.

Technological advances
- Walturdaw introduced their Cinematophone System, which synchronised gramophone recordings with film images.

1912

Censorship of moving images varied from nation to nation, but since the commercial launch of cinema there had been widespread concern at the nature of material appearing on the cinema screen. Religious and moral campaigners had long sought government regulation of the industry; in Britain the industry responded by initiating a system of self-regulation. The British Board of Film Classification (BBFC) was established under the chairmanship of Mr G. A. Redford. It began classification of films for public performance in Britain in 1913, when it examined over 7,000 films, distinguishing between 'A' films deemed suitable only for adults and 'U' films suitable for all ages.

Technological advances
- The Gevaert company of Belgium began to produce coloured film bases onto which films could be directly printed to achieve a tinted effect without the need to dye them after development.
- The Bell and Howell studio camera was launched and, in various forms, became the industry standard for most of the twentieth century.

Industry developments
- Carl Laemmle formed the Universal Film Manufacturing Company, which later became Universal Films.
- Travelling showmen in the UK began to abandon their fairground Bioscope shows and started establishing permanent, static cinemas.

1913

In the US, the system of vertical integration, in which large film companies owned all levels of film production, distribution and exhibition, became increasingly consolidated in California. D. W. Griffith had begun extensive film production in California during 1910 and triggered the migration of New York studios to the area eventually known as Hollywood. The larger film studios' stranglehold on the business left other producers little access to the US market. Georges Méliès, and many of the early pioneers, were increasingly withdrawing from film production. Their importance within the industry would be finally eradicated by World War One.

Industry developments
- The London Film Co. opened studios in Twickenham
- Georges Méliès was declared bankrupt and ceased film production.

1914

Over the previous twenty years, cinema had progressed from little more than a novelty, developed independently in a series of Western countries, to a fully-fledged modern industry. Initially designed for use within diverse pre-existing institutions, cinema had successfully developed as an institution in its own right and had outgrown a whole series of performance and storytelling traditions. In many respects, this point of transition marks the end of the period of early cinema and the beginning of a canon described by film historians as the 'Classical period' of silent cinema. The notion of classicism is characterised by easily understood, well-balanced, and star-driven cinema, exemplified by the increasingly dominant Hollywood studios. In Europe, the outbreak of World War One dramatically stalled the development of national film industries. In Britain the industry arguably never found the momentum it had generated in the preceding decade; it emerged drastically under-financed and became increasingly dependent on foreign films.

Industry developments
- Charlie Chaplin, perhaps still the world's most recognisable film star, began to make films for Keystone in the US.
- The release of the Italian film, *Cabiria*, directed by Giovani Pastrone, set new standards in the scale and spectacle of the moving picture. At ten reels and two-and-a-half hours in length, it marked not only the ascendancy of the feature film but the birth of the epic.

2 APPROACHES TO EARLY CINEMA

Why study early cinema?

> That the present boom in these animated palsy-scopes cannot last
> for ever is a fact that the great majority of people seem to be losing
> sight of altogether, and yet it is only common sense to suppose
> that it will not be so very long before the great British Public gets
> tired of the uncomfortably jerky photographs.
>
> — Cecil Hepworth, 'On the Lantern Screen',
> *The Amateur Photographer* (6 November 1896)

Cecil Hepworth, an important early cinema pioneer, was one of a number
of commentators to predict the untimely demise of moving pictures. His
pessimism, rooted in the firm conviction that 'animated palsy-scopes'
were nothing but a passing fancy, ignored the profound and international
impact that this new medium had already occasioned. By November 1896,
cinema was already developing beyond the status of a scientific curiosity
and entertainment novelty, and Hepworth would quickly revise his
judgment. In a series of parallel developments across the industrialised
world, cinema began to assume multiple existences. Its social, economic,
political and aesthetic impact were to revolutionise public life in a dynamic
range of contexts.

The continued existence of cinema in a digital age is testimony to its unique qualities and capacity to adapt to multiple contexts across decades and national boundaries. Cinema's adaptability, unimaginable for Hepworth in 1896, is one of its most exciting qualities and has attracted concerted academic interest at key historical points in its development. Early cinema represents one of these key points and its study has subsequently developed as an academic discipline in its own right. This period offers us, as scholars, the opportunity to study an unprecedented and enthralling body of textual and contextual material with profound consequences for our contemporary media-saturated society. Early cinema represents a site of extraordinary exchange between audiences and the visual text, which has fascinated historians of popular and visual culture for the last century. No longer subsumed within the broader academic agenda of film studies, early cinema studies has embraced historical, sociological and cultural methodologies which seek to understand early cinema in all of its multiple contexts.

Critical approaches

As part of the process of studying early cinema it is important to understand the traditions in scholarship that inform our current readings of the subject. The history of the subject reveals a series of tensions between traditionally distinctive areas of study such as technology, aesthetics, audiences and business which scholars have only recently begun to synthesise. As part of this process, the relationships between other contemporary media forms such as literature, drama, photography, the press and early cinema are becoming central to our understanding. We shall characterise new approaches to correcting these tendencies as a contemporary revisionist programme. This programme has sought to shift the historical focus from the tradition of a developmental model of cinema to a more inclusive and expanding agenda of positioning cinema within broader notions of media and cultural histories. Both approaches have their benefits and also limitations, and currently these are at an exciting point of interrogation as we move towards the development of more inclusive forms of historical enquiry.

As a means of understanding our current point of departure we offer a brief consideration of traditions within the context of the study of early cinema.

Technological determinism

The first histories of cinema concerned themselves almost exclusively with the development of the technology that made moving pictures possible. These contemporary accounts worked backwards from the realisation of the moving image, through a series of developments in the diverse fields of optics, photochemistry and engineering, to demonstrate that the cinema had evolved in a linear fashion. In effect, these histories were predicated on a historical model concerned with getting from A to Z, from the lens to the cinematograph, via a series of technological advancements.

If we look at contemporary accounts, such as those to be found in the trade journals *The British Journal of Photography* and *The Optical Magic Lantern Journal and Photographic Enlarger*, we can chart the impact of the new medium of film. What is apparent in these accounts is an uncertainty about how to classify cinema and the tendency to represent it as an adaptation of pre-existing technologies. As a consequence, cinema is regarded as belonging to pre-existing technologies and is implicitly judged by existing conventions. For example, early developments in photography from the 1840s were considered purely as antecedents for the eventual realisation of moving photographic images. Similarly, the magic lantern show, in which images were projected onto a screen, prefigured the conventions of projection and screen practice associated with the cinema. Indeed, writers frequently alluded to a much older classical tradition, in which the camera obscura, shadow theatre, and optical toys are seen as direct linear antecedents for various aspects of the cinematographic mechanism. To quote Charles Jenkins, writing for the *Photographic* Times in 1898:

There is one thing that has probably impressed itself upon those who have studied the subject, i.e. That the moving picture machines which have been so widely exploited during the past two years are the culmination of a very long series of experiments. The sensational appearance of these machines in a relatively perfect form has given rise to the general impression that they are something new under the sun, a source of Minerva birth of inventive genius, but like all notable achievements in mechanism the animated picture machine has a long line of predecessors, and the difficult problem of recording and reproducing motion has not yielded without much preliminary fumbling. (C. Jenkins 1898)

It was inconceivable for Jenkins, and other writers, to dissociate the history of cinema from the histories of these predecessors. Cinema was regarded as a linear improvement of the capabilities of the technologies from which it emerged. Such critical orientations privileged technical and scientific issues, and evolved in subsequent formulations into a fully realised model of technological determinism. We can define this model as the means by which technology and technological change are seen as the primary determining factor in the development of the medium.

This approach became entrenched through narrative histories produced by institutions, such as museums and archives, which housed the technological evidence of the development of cinema. As early as 1897, Robert W. Paul, another important British pioneer, was offering to deposit prototypes of his Animatographe with the Science Museum in London:

Sir, I have three instruments which were the original experimental models of the Animatographe, which I shall be pleased to present to the Museum for deposit in the patent branch, if they can be accepted. Awaiting the favour of your reply, I am, Sir, your obedient servant.
    – Robert Paul (15 May 1897)

Institutions such as the Science Museum popularised histories of cinema based on the technological record. Their legacy has been a fascination with the cinema's technological processes of recording and projection, and with subsequent developments, such as the introduction of sound and colour cinematography. Thus, the study of film technology has concentrated upon the contrivance of new mechanical and technical devices in the projection of the moving image, and has described what Laurent Mannoni has called a 'spiral of inventions' (1995: 13). In this model, technological and scientific advances determine aesthetic development and, therefore, entail sociological consequences. For example, according to this model, the development of the story film in the years before 1910 was primarily a response to the invention of technologies of film editing, and it was this influence which brought about the market dominance of the feature film.

Early accounts of the invention of cinema, such as Cecil Hepworth's *ABC of the Cinematograph* (1897) and Henry Hopwood's *Moving Pictures: How they are Made and Worked* (1899), which are among the first cinema histories proper, are predicated on this model of technological determinism. However, the question of causation, for example what triggers technological advance, is not considered in this formative period nor is the relation of technology to aesthetics discussed. Other consequences of this model of technological change are the high esteem in which technology is held and the tendency to regard all developments as positive. This tendency is still discernible, particularly in general histories of early cinema, and characterises influential texts such as Olive Cook's *Movement in Two Dimensions* (1963), C. W. Ceram's *Archaeology of the Cinema* (1965), and Brian Coe's *History of Movie Photography* (1981). Such texts provide valuable source material and are useful in contextualising classical cinema as the product of earlier technological advances. They offer a readily available and seductive narrative of cinematic advances, in which the role of technology is central, and the fully realised feature film of the 1930s and 1940s is the logical conclusion.

The great man theory

The tendency to see cinema's invention and subsequent technological development as the result of the brilliance and sacrifice of a small group of dedicated men led immediately to the personalisation of early cinema history and the proliferation of biographical histories fuelled by the desire to establish and capitalise on the primacy of invention. The process of personalisation that was characterised by Allen and Gomery as 'the Great Man theory' (1985: 51) was often instigated by the personalities themselves. For example, Robert W. Paul and Birt Acres conducted an increasingly antagonistic debate through the letter page of the *British Journal of Photography* throughout 1896 regarding their role in the invention of cinematography in Britain. Their concern was to establish personal recognition for their contribution to cinema, to safeguard their legal status and to exploit the patent rights for cinematographic equipment. All new inventions could be protected from piracy provided they had been registered with the patent office in respective countries, and large incomes could be generated from the granting of licences to second parties. The public spat between Paul and Acres typifies contemporary discourses that tended to personalise the invention of moving pictures. In 1904, Paul published his own account of the development of the Animatographe in one of his trade catalogues, the *Supplementary List of Improved Apparatus for Optical Projection*. The tradition of biographical histories was thus instigated in the interests of self-promotion by the personalities themselves and consequently presents an extremely partial reading of early cinema history. Perhaps the best known of these accounts in the UK is Cecil Hepworth's *Came the Dawn* (1951), which presents a very romanticised account of his contribution to early British cinema.

On an international scale, claims relating to the invention of cinema have tended to follow patriotic lines, with popular pioneer figures from France, the US, Britain and Germany all accredited with the development of the 'first' moving picture apparatus. These claims speak powerfully of parallel developments in the technology of mass media across the Western industrial world, but there is little justification for accrediting responsibility for cinematic invention to any one nation or individual. This question has dominated discussion of early cinema, and has narrowed the range of themes and approaches for a large part of the twentieth century. Indeed, nationalistic defences of particular pioneer figures have detracted from a more nuanced account of the exchanges and cultural specificities of national cinemas.

The 'Great Figures' approach has established a canon, comparable to that associated with established disciplines such as English Literature, which has tended to exclude individuals whose importance was less readily apparent, or who were less adept at self-publicity. It has allowed a series of film historians to accredit responsibility for material advances in film technology and form to a list of famous personalities. Such an approach might be useful in understanding the business practices and aesthetic sensibilities of individual inventors or practitioners. For example, the celebration of Thomas Edison as inventor and businessman, in a wide range of biographical texts, has revealed as much about American capitalism at the turn of the twentieth century as it has about the various forms of work and individual creativity associated with the production of moving pictures. The first major history of American cinema, Terry Ramsaye's *A Million and One Nights: A History of the Motion Picture through 1925* (1926), cements Edison's position as the father of the motion picture and ignores his reputation as an avaricious and ruthless businessman.

While technological and biographical histories have dominated the study of early cinema between the 1890s and the 1970s, they were not the only perspectives in evidence during this period. Important transitional work was undertaken by a disparate group of historians working on survey histories of cinema technologies, aesthetics and commerce. Their perspective was much more inclusive and less partial than that of their contemporaries. In the context of British cinema, two major series of books mark the transition from the purely technological and biographical approaches and prefigure the revisionist project beginning in the 1980s. Rachael Low and Roger Manvell's seminal *History of British Film 1896–1906* (1949) demonstrated the value of a systematic approach to the history of national cinema, shedding light on production, distribution and exhibition practices. Although inevitably incomplete in terms of its coverage of early British film, it demonstrated the benefits of an inclusive approach, linking institutional interests with the aesthetic properties of the films themselves.

John Barnes' exhaustive five-volume account of the years 1894–1901 in the British film industry (*The Beginnings of Cinema in England*) focused not only on the technological development during this period, but also on movie company history, film production and exhibitors. This series is particularly characterised by its inclusion of lesser-known personalities, film companies and engineers, and by its use of trade papers, local newspapers and archive materials. It represents a substantial advance in terms of its rigorous research and scrupulous attention to empirical detail, for example in the inclusion of detailed filmographies. It also signalled key areas of debate concerning early film that had largely been neglected, such as the economics of film manufacture. These were areas of study that would prove increasingly significant for revisionist historians from the 1980s.

Revisionist histories

The birth of early film history as a substantial academic discipline is often cited as a consequence of the 1978 Brighton FIAF conference, in which a large collection of early films were screened for the benefit of delegates. A subsequent process of re-evaluation or revision, applying approaches largely derived from the modern discipline of film studies and textual analysis, generated a series of publications and conferences with ramifications both for the study of early film and for film studies in general. The initial products of this academic reappraisal of early films were a series of readings of film texts, some of which had not been viewed before, and which began to address the cultural and sociological contexts that had occasioned them. The 1980s saw the publication of several important books that championed new approaches from fields as diverse as narrative theory, psychoanalysis, performance theory, aesthetics and gender studies. Michael Chanan's *The Dream that Kicks* (1980) offered an ambitious and multi-disciplinary approach to early cinema, including consideration of the invention of cinema, its performance contexts, its relationships with other popular cultural forms, class dynamics, business practices and spectators. It demonstrated that the study of early cinema would have to address multiple fields of influence and that a number of academic frameworks pertinent to this project were already in place in the broader field of film studies. Similarly, throughout the 1980s, Noël Burch's rigorous formal and analytical approach to early film spectatorship produced a body of work, eventually published in 1990 as *Life to those Shadows* (1990), which owed much to Marxist and psychoanalytical strategies of analysis. This volume offered a comprehensive survey of early film language and theorised that this language followed substantially different conventions from those already associated with classical Hollywood cinema.

Chanan and Burch were not alone in this period in their articulation of the essential difference between early and later film. Indeed, to some extent, Thomas Elsaesser's influential volume of collected essays, *Early Cinema: Space Frame Narrative* (1990) is devoted to an articulation of precisely what it was that was so different about the early cinema and also evidenced the growing range of approaches to the early period. The revisionist programme initiated a range of developing approaches, which we now summarise.

Formal approaches

Formal analysis, in the field of cinema studies, is the interrogation of the fundamental structural characteristics of a film text. It examines aspects of film form such as framing, shot structure and narrative articulation, and is closely associated both with aesthetic criticism and analysis of strategies of staging, filming and editing. It developed as part of film studies in relation to classical and post-classical cinema, and has been extended to early cinema. One of its key exponents has been Barry Salt who has conducted the most extensive chronological analysis of film form to date. Explicitly opposing himself to the mainstream of the revisionist programme, Salt describes himself in his most important work, *Film Style and Technology: History and Analysis* (1992) as a 'practical film theorist'. His perspective has triggered an extensive consideration of early film form, whose ramifications are still being played out:

My overview of the rapid developments in the formal aspects of film in these early years sees some analogies with biological evolution in the way that some novel features which suddenly appear like mutations are sometimes rapidly taken up by other films, forming a line of descent, while on other occasions original devices die out because they have some unsuitability of a technical, commercial, or artistic nature. This approach tends to put the emphasis on what most films come to be like, providing a descriptive norm. (Salt 1990: 31)

Salt argues that a thorough contextual understanding of early film history should be sacrificed in order to achieve a coherent textual understanding of 'what films come to be like'. In Salt's eloquent chronology, which charts technical and formal developments, he identifies the first appearances of innovations in film form that would subsequently become part of the conventions of film language. By contrast, those innovations that were not successful, such as stereoscopic films, are rejected as 'evolutionary dead-ends' of little significance to the greater project of film history (1990: 31). For the student of classical cinema, Salt's formal approach introduces a narrative history in which single shot movies were gradually supplanted by multi-scene films, sophisticated shot transitions and complex narratives. He thus offers a rationale for the appearance of apparently arbitrary conventions of film-making and spectatorship, arguing that they had gradually evolved in accordance with a specified cultural and economic environment. Furthermore, since a significant minority of early films still survive and may be viewed relatively easily by students through increasingly accessible archive networks in Europe and the US, Salt also offers a coherent research methodology to students. A simple assessment of the formal properties of these films can give us some indication of their value as 'evidence' for the early evolution of classical film.

In contrast to Salt's account of film form, Deac Rossell's recent account of the nineteenth-century origins of the movies has advocated a 'non-linear approach' to the history of early cinema, which he believes is able to account for 'seemingly conflicting and contradictory developments' in the technology of moving pictures (Rossell 1998: 10). Instead of attempting to isolate a linear history of development, to which only selected films make a contribution, Rossell suggests that we must also pay close attention to Salt's evolutionary dead-ends if we are to generate a balanced understanding of early film culture. Rossell argues that early film developed unevenly across many parallel paths, and if we choose to consider only one path we sacrifice potentially fascinating and productive fields of study. Rossell's approach is indicative of a revision of the role of technology in cinematic development and is, in fact, consistent with the mainstream of recent revisionist work, which has sought to uncover the multiple functions served by the moving picture in the early period. In doing so, revisionist historians have suggested that, far from being a mere precursor to the feature film, early film constituted a highly sophisticated response to the demands of its contemporary audiences.

A primitive cinema?

Our preconception that films should give us all the information we need in order to consistently interpret them, and to do so in an effortless and economic fashion, remains profoundly unsatisfied by the majority of early films. All too frequently, the modern spectator of early film perceives only the inconsistencies of a poorly manufactured narrative, and the films themselves retain value only in their status as historical artefacts. Without a wide range of contextual knowledge, the small fraction of early films that still survive are of limited value. At best, such films are often interpreted, as in Salt's analysis, as progressional steps towards more sophisticated story films.

In fact, the majority of traditional film criticism has supported this understanding of early film as merely a precursor to the fully developed 'classical' cinema. Although such critics have differed widely about the most appropriate definition of classicism, most have agreed with film theorist André Bazin in his assertion that, 'if cinema in its cradle lacked all the attributes of cinema to come, it was with reluctance and because its fairy guardians were unable to provide them however much they would have liked to' (Bazin 1967: 21). Early films are therefore to be considered primitive and poorly realised examples of the camera's ability to capture a simple chain of events and tell sophisticated stories. They exemplify the beginning of film's development into the dominant twentieth-century storytelling medium. According to this point of view, film is considered to have inevitably evolved from what Burch described as early film's 'Primitive Mode of Representation' (PMR) to the sophisticated 'Institutional Mode of Representation' (IMR) typified by the Hollywood cinema (Burch 1990: 186–202).

However, in the past 25 years, the evolutionary model has been criticised from a series of academic perspectives. In particular, the supposed primitivity of early film has been called into question by critics, including Burch, who has argued that the PMR need not be seen as a mere stepping stone to classical cinema. This movement can be seen as a response to film historian Charles Musser's definitive proposal in an article of 1979 that, 'early cinema [should] be examined within the context of a history of the screen, of the projected image and its sound accompaniment' (Musser 1979: 3). If film form was relatively simple in the years before 1910, such accounts argue, exhibition strategies for film were remarkably sophisticated and diverse. Therefore, in order to effectively interpret early films, we must address the specific conditions of their exhibition and reception.

Subsequently, exhibition practices have increasingly taken centre stage in the academic arena. Already, our growing understanding of early film audiences has shown that, far from an undeveloped and primitive medium, early film can be seen as the apex of nineteenth-century entertainments – even as the epitome of representational media at the fin-de-siècle. From this perspective even a formally simple early film, like the Lumière comedy *L'arroseur arosé* (1895), comprising only one shot of less than a minute, represents an effective response to the sophisticated demands of contemporary exhibitors and audiences. The subject, a well-known visual gag in which a gardener is fooled into looking down the nozzle of a hosepipe and is subsequently drenched, proved a popular film subject. The film played on the audiences' knowing response to the gag, a sophisticated interaction that relied on audience expectation and anticipation of the punch line. The film's success led to widespread emulation: the Bamforth company, for example, produced a version entitled *The Biter Bit* in 1900, which replicated the original almost exactly. Evidencing relationships between films and audiences is most effectively achieved through close readings of contemporary accounts and reviews of film shows. We now offer an example and close reading of such a review.

Case study: opening of the Lumière show at the Empire Theatre, Edinburgh (1 June 1896) and the factory gate film

The Lumières toured their Cinématographe across Europe in the early months of 1896, appointing agents in each country to represent their company and exhibit Cinématographe films. The magician and shadow artist, Felicien Trewey, was appointed in the UK, and premiered a show to an invited audience at The Regent Street Polytechnic on 20 February 1896. The following evening the show opened to the public at the Marlborough Hall, Regent Street Polytechnic and ran until 14 July. Trewey also toured with the Cinématographe during this period, visiting Edinburgh for two weeks:

> The management of the Empire has made a distinct hit. Last night everything worked with perfect smoothness. The Cinématographe, seen in its full perfection, seemed to come to the audience as something of a revelation. When the first of the series of pictures appeared on the screen they applauded heartily, and as one picture after another was exhibited their enthusiasm grew. The management of the light was perfect; the movement of the figures was wonderfully natural; and the general effect was singularly pleasing. The series opened with a view representing the dinner hour at a factory gate at Lyons, in which the hurry and bustle of the operatives leaving their work at mid-day was admirably depicted. A most effective view was the arrival of the Paris mail at an intermediate station; in another the troubles of a photographer with

a fidgety patron was admirably hit off. Particularly attractive also, was the representation full of life and movement of the Champs Elysees; and the sea pieces were wonderfully fine. Altogether, the Cinématographe under Mons. Trewey's direction proved one of the greatest attractions which has been seen at the Empire for some time, and the audience were so enthusiastic in their applause that the curtain was raised and a beautiful sea-scape under moonlight, the waves dashing upon the rocks, was shown. (*The Scotsman*, 2 June 1896)

This review offers us an intriguing glimpse into the way the early Lumière shows were conducted and suggests too the appreciation with which this audience met the show. In June 1896, the moving picture was still a novelty for most audiences outside of London, and the revelation of 'wonderfully natural' movement appearing onscreen was certainly a prime attraction. Indeed, for early audiences, the spectacle of the Cinématographe itself and of the wonder of moving images projected onto a screen was more significant than the content of the films themselves. The mere appearance of waves breaking on the shore was an especially attractive spectacle for this reviewer. Among the films mentioned in this review, the opening *La Sortie des Ouvriers de l'usine Lumière* (1895) became one of the most emulated films of the period, perhaps because an audience largely drawn from working-class backgrounds felt an affinity for its subject. The film, which depicts the Lumières' own workers exiting the factory, runs for less than a minute and employs neither camera movement nor editing. It arguably exemplifies the PMR, essentially presenting to audiences little more than a fixed tableau, a moving photograph. Indeed, it was common practice to begin a show with a still frame which was then cranked into life by the projectionist. Yet, these films, which would become known as 'factory gate' films, were produced well into the 1910s and were often exhibited for the benefit of local audiences who would be drawn to film shows by the prospect of seeing themselves depicted on-screen. For example, the Mitchell and Kenyon Company in the UK were among several companies who specialised in producing factory gate films for local exhibitors. The following extract from a Hepworth and Co. advertisement of 1901 clearly evidences the appeal of such films for early audiences:

To Showmen.
The most popular Cinematograph Film in a Travelling Show is ALWAYS A LOCAL PICTURE containing Portraits which can be recognised. A Film showing workers leaving a factory will gain far greater popularity in the town where it was taken than the most exciting picture ever produced. The workers come in hundreds, with all their friends and relations, and the Film more than pays for itself the first night. In other words this is The Greatest Draw you can have and it is Our Business to Provide it for you in Advance, for each Town you visit. (*The Showman*, August 1902)

Travelling to each town before the film exhibitor arrived there, the Hepworth Co. produced films with a unique local appeal for audiences. The obvious success of such formally simple films therefore depended on a surprisingly sophisticated relationship with audiences and an appreciation of modes of spectatorship. This relationship between disparate audiences, film exhibitors and film producers can be used to counter notions of primitivism in early cinema and demonstrates that early film shows were already engaged in a complex exchange with their audiences. Evidence of these exchanges can be found in reviews of local shows in this period:

The annual fair and statute which was held on the 2nd, 3rd and 4th of November, generally provides a genuine success all round. The weather was very unsettled, but nevertheless good business was done, and the ground was well-filled with shows and roundabouts, including Lawrence's world-famed electrograph, which you might say was topping the bill. The big draw was a local film of the Belper mill hands leaving work; and I must say it was rather amusing to be inside when they were showing this one, as you kept hearing the refrain (*ad lib.*), 'O there's our Mary!' 'O, that's little Sally Smith!' etc. (*The Showman*, December 1900)

The dominant model suggested by the PMR tends to obscure notions of audience sophistication and often leaves the impression that audiences were extremely naïve. However, this reviewer expresses a rather knowing attitude and demonstrates that not all spectators watched early films in the same way.

Intermediality and intertextuality

Increasingly we are studying early cinema within the context of other types of representation and other media forms in an attempt to understand its position within notions of a new visual culture. We also seem to be moving away from discrete areas of historical investigation and towards the development of interpretive models which allow for the positioning of early cinema within an all-embracing notion of a new mass visual culture specific to the end of the nineteenth century. Any understanding of the nature and complexity of this new culture demands an approach which examines film texts in relation to other photographic, dramatic, literary and journalistic texts. Traditionally, our sense of intermedial relationships in early cinema, that is, those between early cinema and different representational forms, has concentrated on technological similarities. For example, the tendency to examine mechanical and chemical relationships between cinema and ocular technologies such as lenses, optical toys and photography, often characterised as pre-cinematic, has obscured more inclusive and revealing relationships.

We can investigate these relationships, which were often integral to the film text, through a number of perspectives which relate to notions of narrative and aesthetic form, performance traditions and conventions, representation, commercial exploitation, ideological content and notions of multi-media entertainment (See Popple & Toulmin 2000).

Intertextuality, a term derived from the work of literary theorists, describes the multiple relationships between the content of texts. Traditionally, film historians have focused on the intertextual transference of specific narratives and genres from one medium to another and have examined how those narratives have been adapted to suit film exhibition

Anonymous postcard of early British Open Air Studio (c. 1905) demonstrating the close relationship between stage and screen.

practices. For example, in the case of literary texts, film historians have concentrated upon the adaptation to the screen of classic literary narratives, such as the plays of Shakespeare or the novels of Charles Dickens, during the 1910s. In this period, these well-established texts played a significant part in bringing about a gentrification of the picture theatres. Seeking to attract increasingly middle-class and wealthy audiences, the classic literary text provided the film industry with a sense of intellectual and highbrow credibility. The intermedial and intertextual mode of study thus tends to present a linear model which follows narratives through a series of progressive historical media developments. Whilst this is often illuminating and highlights specific practices, it also often ignores the dynamic interplay between co-existing media.

We can begin to investigate some of these contiguous relationships through cinema's representation of specific historical events and, perhaps, observe it as acting or re-acting to events. We can examine the ways in which cinematic representations offer different perspectives or merely replicate established patterns of representation created by other media forms.

Case study: representing the Boers

The Anglo-Boer War, fought between 1899–1902, offers a prime example of the inter-play between early cinema and other media 'attractions', including the news press, satirical images and advertising, music hall, theatre, and patriotic entertainments (see Popple 2002).

Photographic and cinematic images were central to providing a visual representation of the conflict, providing a new technological iconography of the war, which replaced more traditional forms of print journalism and images created by the war artist. New media, based predominantly on the technologies of the camera and the telegraph, accelerated the delivery of images and determined their very nature.

The cinema acted as an interface between these media and absorbed narrative concerns and traditions of performance to achieve its status as the key mediator of the war at home. A central narrative concerned the nature and conduct of the Boers, and their behaviour on the field of battle was obsessively contrasted with that of the British Tommy (Popple 2002: 17).

Racial stereotypes of the Boers were a perpetual feature of a range of media products, and themes relating to hygiene, conduct and decency were constantly referred to throughout the course of the war. Advertising campaigns commissioned for brands like Monkey Brand Soap were illustrated by pictorial representations of dirty Boer troops and many satirical references were made to their lack of personal hygiene. Another prominent narrative of the war concerned abuses of military conventions, and atrocity stories were constantly reported. The Boers were accused of poisoning drinking water, using poisoned bullets, attacking ambulances, mistreating their prisoners and abusing the white flag. Reports of 'White Flag' incidents, when British troops were attacked by troops pretending to surrender, became commonplace in 1900, and the press accounts were quickly represented in a range of literary, pictorial and cinematic narratives which focused on British decency and the Boer abuses.

The Mitchell and Kenyon Company began to produce a range of patriotic propaganda films in 1900 that invoked many of these narratives. Their subjects were familiar to anyone with a passing acquaintance with other contemporary texts: *White Flag Treachery* (1900), *Shelling the Red Cross* (1900), *A Sneaky Boer* (1900), *Washing Boer Prisoners* (*Washing A Boer Prisoner in Camp*, 1900) and *Poisoning the Well* (1901). These films demonstrate a sense of complex and developing relationships between early cinema and a range of other media texts.

An archaeology of cinema?

The complexities revealed by intertextual and intermedial analyses of early cinema raise a key methodological problem for scholars. How is it possible to inclusively describe a range of film-making and film viewing practices that are definitively disparate? One group of film historians has responded to this difficulty by instigating a series of micro-historical studies dedicated to individual film-makers, film exhibitors, exhibition sites or important events. Taken as a whole, this revisionist historical approach has radically improved our understanding of early film culture. By looking at the sites and events for which substantial records are still in existence, we are able to discern a clearer picture of early cinema more generally. Thus, for example, a growing body of work concerning the role of the cinematograph in the World's Fairs at the beginning of the twentieth century has begun to expose a number of hitherto underdeveloped connections between moving pictures representing foreign lands, the museum full of exotic artefacts, and the growing popularity of tourism in the period. Similarly, Charles Musser and Carol Nelson's book-length study of American travelling exhibitor Lyman H. Howe has convincingly demonstrated the importance of the showman's personality to the successful entertainment (Musser & Nelson 1991). Each of these accounts may be regarded as a minute contribution to an 'archaeology' of early film. Altogether, this archaeology is a massive enterprise that has sought to trace the multiple lines of influence on early cinema. Such an approach continues to offer students of early film the opportunity for remarkably specialised historical research in an ever-widening field. One of the chief pleasures in the field is the opportunity to reconstruct, from rare and often unknown sources, the characteristics of individual exhibition sites, individual exhibitors and showmen, and even individual shows. At the same time, accomplished researchers can celebrate their contribution to an overarching history of early film within its own cultural context, and not simply as the primitive origin of classical cinema.

The archaeological approach to early cinema celebrates the disparate and fragmentary nature of its historical sources, but for this reason can also be very frustrating for students new to the field. Micro-historical research is central to contemporary approaches to early cinema, but also requires interpretation within more coherent and systematic frameworks. The *cinema of attractions* model, originally developed by Tom Gunning and André Gaudreault in the context of early North American cinema studies, has been arguably the most successful response to this problem (Gaudreault & Gunning 1989: 49–63).

As Gunning explains, the model of a cinema of attractions is derived from the work of Russian film theorist Sergei Eisenstein, who argued in the 1920s that the ideal film form would consist of a series of disparate and often competing attractions, not unlike the competing attractions of an amusement park (Eisenstein 1988: 39–58). According to Gunning, the cinema of attractions is to be defined in contrast to the story film that later became dominant in US film production. He has variously suggested dates, from 1903–8, as critical moments in the transition from the cinema of attractions to what he calls the 'cinema of narrative integration' (Gunning 1989: 31–45; Gunning 1991: 6). This transition is rather similar to the evolution of film proposed by Burch from PMR to IMR, but the cinema of attractions is not to be regarded as a primitive precursor of a later form. Indeed, in terms of exhibition strategies, the early cinema of attractions is arguably more sophisticated than the cinemas that were to follow. Like the amusement park, the experience was a dynamic collision of competing attractions, where the films were only one part of the performance. We can summarise the principle features of the cinema of attractions as follows:

- The cinema of attractions foregrounds the act of display rather than depending upon a fictional storyline. According to Gunning, it is an 'exhibitionist cinema' that advertises the medium of film as an attraction in its own right (1991: 41). It is therefore exemplified during exhibition by showmen and other live performers, such as magicians, freaks and musicians, whose role during exhibition was to draw the admiring attention of paying customers to the films.
- It exploits the element of 'surprise, shock, and trauma' experienced by audiences rather than the more sedate pleasures associated with the linear unfolding of a storyline (Gunning 1986: 70). Like an attraction in an amusement park, it offers to audiences the possibility for a new and surprising experience.
- It demands an audience's active response to unfamiliar and disturbing material rather than the spectator's passive response to familiar and comfortable material. Unlike the convention of silent spectatorship we expect in modern cinemas, the cinema of attractions encouraged spectators to be noisy and interactive. This

was a cinema for which the spectator, bombarded by a sequence of images onscreen, noisily participated in the production of meaning.

Given the derivation of the term, it is not surprising that the attractionist model has been most convincing when applied to early film shows at sites such as variety theatres and fairgrounds. At these sites, which had traditionally depended on an intriguing blend of exhibitionism, shock, and audience interaction, the film show was, after all, just another attraction. However, in the years since its initial formulation, the cinema of attractions has often served as a rationale for the great volume of recent micro-historical work. The fragmented and often inconsistent nature of such work is easily justified by reference to a model of film exhibition that already celebrates fragmentation and inconsistency. For students, this model usefully suggests that a simple logic underlies seemingly disparate strands of research concerning early cinema.

Conclusion

A number of approaches have been applied to the study of early cinema, all of which have passionate advocates and offer students a coherent reading of an inherently complex subject. As students you will need to be aware of these approaches and will undoubtedly adopt your own perspectives, drawing upon aspects of these traditions. In order to fully appreciate the subtle variations in emphasis and approach, you will need to read as widely as possible across historical and academic boundaries and be prepared to experiment with aspects of often disparate opinion.

3 THE 'USES' OF CINEMA

When we think of early cinema we tend to regard it primarily as a new mass entertainment form, another stage in the development of an increasingly pan-global visual culture. Our responses and interrogative inclinations are to attempt to understand it in isolation and to privilege our understanding of its form, technologies and aesthetic development. What we miss in our initial enthusiasm for this new media are the contexts and conventions which bind it to a broader set of mass media cultures. Our own readings of the film text, for example, are far removed from the lives and responses of cinema's initial consumers and their real life experiences (see Crarey 2001).

As a consequence our contemporary ideological orientations tend to predominate, and we are in danger of becoming disengaged from cinema's original contexts and constituencies. We cannot, obviously, re-create or even successfully re-imagine these conditions fully, but we can study and hypothesise with relative certainty many facets of the early period of cinema. One such area of study resides in our notion of the initial 'uses' of the medium.

The consideration of the uses of the cinematic form in this period opens up a wide-ranging and extremely rich field of study. It encourages us as historians to raise a series of questions about the nature and range of those contexts and to answer a common set of questions about the ownership, regulation, content and consumption of cinema. As John

Tagg has suggested in relation to the photographic image, we need to be constantly aware of questions concerning why images are made, who made them and who consumed them, and what were the conditions under which they were made (1988: 119).

The early cinema, in its multiple guises, was used to perform a number of roles that related directly to diverse social, political, cultural and economic circumstances. Whilst it is dangerous to generalise, as national and even regional conditions varied enormously, we can examine the general uses of the medium as a means of understanding its survival and development. Contemporary reactions to its uses are often equally revealing, as we will now show. The question of regulation, for example, offers a strong insight into specific notions of political, religious and moral orthodoxy, and the series of relationships that developed between cinema and state.

Cinema, state, propaganda and censorship: an ordered society?

The arrival of cinema represented a new technological means of communication with the potential to reach a truly mass audience. Film became increasingly easy to manufacture and disseminate, and seemed destined to draw a swift series of responses from the state as it was increasingly deployed to represent difficult and contentious material.[1] In Britain, however, the first example of direct government intervention in the industry had to wait until 1909. The Cinematograph Act was introduced to protect the safety of cinemagoers at the various venues in which films were exhibited (Harding & Popple 1996: 46–8).

One of the defining moments in the early history of the cinema had been the Paris Charity Bazaar Fire (4 May 1897) in which 121 people perished. The fire was started by an ether lamp at a Cinematograph demonstration and achieved international notoriety because many of those who perished were society figures. The fact that fires and explosions were a common feature of existing magic lantern and theatrical performances that used the same lighting technologies seemed of little importance. Projectionists needed to combine a highly combustible mixture of either oxygen and hydrogen or oxygen and domestic gas to burn in their lime-light lamps to illuminate their shows. These elements were combined from pressurised cylinders in a mixing bag and accidents were a regular occurrence. Fatalities and mutilations were commonplace, exacerbated by the highly flammable nature of nitrate-based early film stock.

The 1909 act charged local councils with the responsibility of licensing all premises for exhibition of films including itinerant and non-theatrical venues. Whilst the act was not primarily used to restrict what audiences actually observed on screen, it was also employed by local authorities as a device to prevent exhibitions. Existing laws such as Lord Campbell's Obscene Publications Act of 1857, aimed at photographic obscenity, could be invoked, yet no formal obscenity act was legislated against the cinema in Britain. The industry – as it later did in the US – opted for a voluntary trade system of self-regulation. The British Board of Film Censors emerged in November 1912 and commenced a programme of classification of films in 1913 that forms the basis of the system still in operation today. Film-makers were under no legal compunction to submit their films for classification, but to refuse could mean exclusion from exhibition in certain areas by powers vested in local councils. This self-regulation, which later became codified, would seem to suggest that cinema was considered an unimportant phenomenon and not worthy of serious state regulatory control. This could not be further from the truth, as many of its uses in this early period unleashed a wave of moral and religious panics that blamed the cinema for growing social problems as diverse as juvenile delinquency, prostitution and atheism. Many commentators began to make direct connections between what was seen on the cinema screen and trends in social behaviour. These debates centred around issues of social conformity, crime, political unrest and broader public morality. The very venues associated with the exhibition of cinema were often characterised as being unsanitary and encouraging immorality. Many of these attacks were class-based, and levelled at venues, particularly the music hall and the transient penny gaff and fairground shows, which were associated with working-class dissolution, drinking, sedition and prostitution. In a survey carried out by the National Council of Public Morals in 1917 Dr

Marie Stopes, pioneer of women's birth control, conducted a number of interviews with children concerning the perceived dangers of cinema.

> *Dr Marie Stopes*: Have you seen any picture which you thought at the time was bad to see?
> *School Child*: No, but I saw a picture once which I thought was vulgar. It was called ––.
> *M.S.*: Supposing you went into a picture house and you met a fairy at the door who told you you could see any picture you like, what kind would you like to see?
> *S.C.*: I should like to see a picture about a circus.
> *M.S.*: What sort of picture would you like best?
> *S.C.*: I should like a good drama, but not a love drama. A nice drama like *Little Miss Nobody* which I thought was very nice.
> *M.S.*: Why don't you like love dramas?
> *S.C.*: There is too much fooling around in them, and there is always hatred between two men and two women.
> *M.S.*: You don't like to see two men hating each other?
> *S.C.*: Well, it is a lot of silliness. I do not think it would happen in real life.
> *M.S.*: You never got any disease at the cinema?
> *S.C.*: No, but once I got scarlet fever, but not in a cinema.
> *M.S.*: Did you ever get anything?
> *S.C.*: No, I did not catch my disease there.[2]

However, social commentators also advocated the use of cinema as a means of social instruction. The cinema thus operated between these twin poles of moral condemnation and moral improvement. Much of the rich evidence of these debates lies in the contemporary press, and even a cursory survey provides us with a rich commentary concerning the effects of films on their spectators. The question of media effects remains as contentious today as it has always been, and evidence of this particular debate is well represented by the press. These following two extracts from *The Times* in 1913 and 1914 illustrate a common set of perceptions:

Judge on Picture Shows

At the London Session yesterday Mr. Wallace, dealing with the case of a boy who pleaded guilty to burglary, said he believed that cinematograph shows were responsible for the downfall of many young people. Many of the lads who came before him owed their position to having been influenced by pictures of burglaries and thefts at such shows ... These shows, as far as young boys were concerned, were a grave danger to the community. (Anon. 1913a)

The Cinema and the Young

A number of young lads were before the Sutton Coldfield magistrates yesterday charged with a series of thefts, and the assertion was made that their appearance in the dock was largely due to the harmful influence of certain picture theatres. In several cases the lads were bound over not to enter a picture theatre for 12 months. The Chairman said the town had been made notorious as a den of young thieves and shopkeepers had been terrorised. A petition, signed by clergy and ministers of religion and by the local branch of the Women's Temperance Association, was presented, suggesting the closer supervision of picture theatres. They urged that no picture should be allowed to be shown which represented violence and wrongdoing, and objected to certain posters. (Anon. 1914)

Both reports actively promote the notion that there is a direct relationship between the cinema and criminal activity in the minds of the judiciary and certain sections of British society. But whilst they demonstrate these perceptions within a highly stratified social system, they should not be read as direct evidence of the effects of cinema. As a historical source they can be read as evidence of a particular social reaction to the cinema and the imposition of certain moral, social, and by extension, political standards. The second extract explicitly identifies the groups involved in this campaign as judicial, religious and property-owning. We can further read these texts as examples of a class-based response to cinema, one which clearly identifies young, working-class males as susceptible to temptation. Other targets, particularly women and children, are also commonly identified in similar texts. Such reports have a tendency to generalise about cinema, and largely ignore specific films, referring to generic types as problematic. It is, however, often possible to relate the dates of specific offences to listings in the press in order to determine which films were being screened in a particular area, and which might have formed the basis of the case.

Socially protective groups, such as the Church, often attempted to counter the perceived corrupting influences of cinema by using it as a form of proselytisation for their own causes and applying it to moral campaigns such as the temperance movement. Unlike the Catholic Church, which, for a while, banned Priests from attending picture houses,[3] the Salvation Army was one of the earliest advocates of the beneficial role of the cinema, establishing its own Cinematograph Department in 1897. In this context the cinema could not only present wholesome and religious subjects to an audience, but on a more practical level kept them out of temptation's way in the public house or music hall. As leisure time increased, so did the potential for antisocial behaviour, and many religious organisations overcame their opposition to the Sunday opening of cinemas, considering it a lesser evil than having the working classes on the streets once they had left church. As one Salvation Army officer commented in 1906:

> As to laughter and merriment, God meant His people to be happy, and, just as the devil has no right to all the best music – let alone the 'catchy' tunes – no more has he any right to a monopoly of pictures grave and gay, or modern improvements on the magic lantern of our youth, which used to show us highly coloured views. (Anon. 1906)

In the same way that films could be used to advance social and moral agendas, they could also provide commentary on contentious political issues such as votes for women. The women's suffrage movement was particularly active in this period and became the subject of several films before World War One. Probably the earliest of these suffrage films was the Bamforth/Riley Brothers film *Women's Rights*, produced c. 1899. The film depicts two women having their skirts nailed to a fence whilst discussing women's rights. Later series of films included *Lady Barber* (1905), *Sweet Suffragette* (1906), *She Would be A Suffragette* (1908), *A Suffragette in spite of Himself* (1912) and *Selina's Flight for Freedom* (1914). Perhaps the most interesting of these films is Clarendon's film of 1913, *Milling The Militants*.

The film follows the fortunes of a militant Suffragette and her daydreaming chauvinistic husband. Its depiction of the suffrage movement is deeply stereotyped, the women presented as violent and distinctly unfeminine. In a series of dream sequences the women are punished for daring to demand the vote by being made to wear male clothes, dig the road, smoke pipes and undergo the ordeal of the ducking stool. Yet, as the synopsis from the *Kine Weekly* suggests and the film evidences, it is also a social comedy in which the women have the last laugh:

> The spouse of a suffragette has a sad experience after dreaming dreams of suppressing his better half – Brown is blessed with a large wife and a small family, whom he is left to look after while his better half goes forth armed with a hammer to smash, burn and plunder. Brown falls asleep and dreams that he is Prime Minister and making laws to suppress the militants. Brown is gloating over a recalcitrant female when he is awakened, and his wife is upsetting a pail of water over him, at the same time scolding him for sleeping and neglecting his duties. His courage fails him, and the late 'Prime minister' begs for mercy on his knees. (in Harding & Popple 1996: 44)

Such synopses are often the only sources available for films that are either lost or in inaccessible archives, and can offer us limited scope for interpretation. This is a particular problem associated with early cinema as the vast majority of films produced during this period have not survived and were not systematically collected until the international film archive movement got into its stride in the 1930s. Those films preserved in archives are often incomplete or exist in different versions which can be restored, or at least imagined, using the synopses or reviews of early films that can be found in the specialist trade press of the time. However, these useful descriptions only developed fully after the turn of the century, and earlier descriptions must be traced from production and distribution catalogues, or from local newspaper reviews. It is often impossible to uncover more than a title and a brief description of a film, so our interpretation of this information requires careful consideration.

In the case of *Milling the Militants* we are able to combine both film and a contemporary account in order to suggest a reading of social attitudes towards female emancipation and to demonstrate the use of cinema as a form of social commentary. We can also gauge contrary reactions by consulting a wide range of periodicals that often demonstrated very specific social and political agendas of their own. The more sources we are able to bring to bear upon a film or group of films, the more convincing and cohesive our interpretation. This also brings into sharp focus the narrative sources of particular films, such as newspapers, satirical representations, and theatrical sketches, which were absorbed into films and often informed the response of increasingly sophisticated and diverse audiences. The social and gender construction of an audience was often a crucial factor in relation to the success of a particular film or performance, and provides a fascinating area of study for the early film scholar.

Science and education

Whilst cinema was often contentiously used as a means of moral and social education, it was increasingly adapted to the fields of scientific research and formal education. As a technological recording device, with the capacity to arrest or accelerate time, cinematography had an immediate impact in the field of scientific research. For example, work conducted by Dr Lucien Bull into high-speed cinematography enabled widespread research into the analysis of insect flight and modern ballistics technology. Much of the potential of cinematography had been demonstrated in the photographic experimentation of researchers such as Eadweard Muybridge, Etienne-

Jules Marey and Georges Demeny (see Braun 1992). These experimenters were engaged in the study of human and animal locomotion and had developed sequential, or chronophotographic, cameras in the 1880s which, like the cine-camera, captured continuous sequences of images which could be subsequently animated. Their physiological studies were dramatically extended by the advent of cinematography, and research extended through the application of slow motion and time-lapse films.

Writing in December 1896, V. E. Johnson outlined a number of scientific applications, which included the identification of criminals, the study of machinery, the recording of the pathologies of disease, the study of meteorology, fluid dynamics, surgery and the flight of birds (Johnson 1896). There were many others who quickly realised the potential of scientific cinematography, and one of the most perceptive was the Pole, Bolesław Matuszewski, a Lumière cameraman and fierce advocate for cinema. In 1898 he published the world's first film manifesto, *Une Nouvelle Source de L'Histoire*, which suggested the establishment of an archive of historical film.[4] In his subsequent publication *La Photographie Animée*, he offered a number of suggestions for the use of cinema in the service of science and education. Indeed he had pioneered the filming of surgery in Warsaw that same year. Surgical films were considered an important development because they offered the potential for formal training, as this early account from 1899 indicates:

The Cinematograph in Surgery
> The animated photographs which for some time have been the delight of thousands of sightseers and holiday-makers in all parts of the civilised world have now appeared in new and, it would seem, a very useful role. A celebrated French surgeon, M. Doyen, has conceived the idea of picturing in this manner the various phases of an operation form the first cut of the knife to the final adjustment of the bandages, each detail of the work being as excellently shown that a mistake could hardly be made by a receptive observer. At a recent demonstration at the University of Kiel, before a select company of doctors and other scientific men,

a complete series of these surgical films were thrown on a screen, and excited great enthusiasm among those present. (Anon. 1899)

The most direct inference is that these films could subsequently be employed to train surgeons, and the role of cinema as educator was commonly advocated. Indeed its power to widen the franchise for education was keenly appreciated. In an article entitled *The Future of the Cinematograph*, written in 1899, Mrs J. E. Whitby outlined this democratic notion:

> To students unable to attend the lectures of the cleverest and ablest professors, as well as those whom fate compels to reside at some distance from the centres of education, the cinematograph in its new function will come as an incalculable boon; for it will be possible by its aid to repeat the illustrative action of the greatest authority on any given subject, and by means of an accompanying lecture to repeat the lesson not only as many times as may be required, but in as many different places. This will enable the poor as well as the rich, the country as well as the town mouse, to enjoy the same high advantages. (Whitby 1900)

Many other educational schemes were mooted including the training of omnibus drivers (Anon. 1913b), and in 1913 the London County Council began a series of experimental film screenings of educational films for children largely depicting living and working conditions in other countries (Anon. 1913c).

The commercial cinema developed in Britain simultaneously with another technological phenomenon, the Röntgen or X-ray, in January 1896. For a brief period both vied with each other as a form of popular entertainment on the music hall stage and fairground booth. Whilst the cinema allowed people to see themselves in motion, the X-ray seemed to allow even more: it allowed them to look inside their own bodies. The novelty of the X-ray as a form of entertainment soon receded and its function as a medical and scientific tool rapidly outstripped its attraction as a scientific novelty. It was subsequently employed in combination with the cine-camera to produce X-ray films which served a serious scientific purpose, but also attracted popular attention (see Crangle 1998). Thus the cinema began a process of popularising science and re-presenting it as education and entertainment.

Various specialist companies began manufacturing popular science titles, employing the latest technologies, such as time-lapse and early colour processes. One in particular, The Charles Urban Trading Company, pioneered the introduction of scientific films with the popular *Unseen World Series* in 1903. The advertising material promised to reveal 'nature's closest secrets'. These popular science and nature films developed rapidly in the 1900s with the work of film-makers such as Cherry Kearton, whose films of exploration, mountaineering and big game hunting included Theodore Roosevelt's African expedition of 1908. But perhaps more than any other film of this type, Herbert Ponting's films of the ill-fated Scott Antarctic expedition of 1911 produced some of the most stunning and alien images the British public had seen.

Worlds within worlds: news and globalisation

Travel and exploration films were symptomatic of the role cinema was playing in diminishing the geographic, scientific and cultural boundaries of the late Victorian and Edwardian world. Cinema was central to the process of globalisation, of making the world a smaller place. The mass of the world's industrial populations had only recently taken for granted the process of self- representation that cheap photography had facilitated. The hierarchical characteristics of visual representation, particularly those predicated on class, gender and ethnicity were transferred from the conventions of photographic practice into cinematographic forms, just as pre-photographic traditions had been assimilated into photographic practice. Yet somehow the sheer scale and nature of consumption altered their potential to engage a new mass audience. The photograph was primarily consumed by the individual within a domestic context; cinema presaged mass, public representation.

As we have already shown, the genre of 'factory gate' films relied on the delight of seeing oneself not only represented but moving on screen, and not only situated the spectator within another space but also, by implication, within the other worlds increasingly represented in that particular space: on the cinema screen. The stasis of the photographic carte and the photograph album was replaced by the living world of the screen. People could observe their own lives and circumstances and draw direct comparisons with circumstances they saw depicted elsewhere. A tension between the 'real' and the 'imagined' often drew unfavourable comparisons and blurred the distinctions between film's power as a realistic document and fictional medium. This was particularly evident in relation to the documentary or news film. The growth of the print press and a news culture in the late nineteenth century allowed film-makers to rapidly assume a leading role in the presentation of 'living newspapers'. The print press had only very recently been able to illustrate their publications with photographic images using the new half-tone process and adult literacy rates, even in industrial centres, were still very low. Whilst the earliest actuality films operated and were often presented as a pseudo-news service specific cinema news companies were soon established and began producing what became known as the newsreel. The first official news cinema in Britain was called the *Daily Bioscope* and opened in London on 23 May 1906. It was followed by the first British newsreel company, the *Topical Budget* in 1911 (see McKernan 1992). However, as we will now see, the reliability and status of the news as it was represented on-screen was often called into question.

Case study: 'sham cinematograph films'

The central question as to whether audiences implicitly accepted cinematic representations of news and actuality subjects as 'real' presents historians of early cinema with a complex problem of interpretation for which direct evidence is largely absent. Attempting to understand how audiences received cinema, and how they interacted with its disparate subjects, is a demanding field of study. However, we can begin to propose models of audience reception derived from specific micro-historical studies of individual performances or performance contexts. One such context which throws questions of realism and verisimilitude to the fore was the representation of conflict. The specific technological and human problems of producing films from distant and dangerous sites of war often precluded the acquisition of actuality footage from the battlefield. One has only to read W. K. L. Dickson's account of filming during the early stages of the Boer War to appreciate the circumstances which increasingly prompted film-makers to manufacture fake footage.

Public demand for cinematic representations of such conflicts was serviced by a competing market of media attractions, which combined to form dynamic nationalistic and patriotic narratives relating to the prosecution of war. The role of cinema within these mass narratives was complex, but central to that role was the diminishing of geographical boundaries and the potential for audiences to see their 'boys' in the field and to demonise their foe. Despite a willingness, evidenced in a multiplicity of advertisements, to present audiences with real footage 'from the seat of war', exhibitors rarely fulfilled their promises. Some, like the Biograph Company and Edison's Waragraph, were offering an actuality-based news service and, in the case of the Waragraph, were using reviews to advertise the impact of their shows:

'The Waragraph' – The stern realities of war have been brought home in very vivid and thrilling fashion to the people of Newcastle-on-Tyne. The exhibitions given by means of the Edison Waragraph in the Olympia have attracted thousands of people, and the movements of the British troops in South Africa, depicted with so much realism, have been followed with breathless interest by the large audiences, whose enthusiasm could not be greater even were they witnessing the actual scenes instead of animated pictures. The pictures are so many and so various that anything like a description is impossible here; all we aim at doing is to advise those few people which have not yet seen them to take advantage of the opportunities afforded this last week of their visit. Most

THE

THOMAS-EDISON

ANIMATED PICTURES

CHINA AND BOER WARS.

Edison's Animated Pictures embraces all parts of the World. Over Ten Thousand are now in Stock, and cannot be surpassed for Clearness, Steadiness, and their absence of Flicker.

Letterhead from Edison's Waragraph (1901).

of the pictures are descriptive of deeds of heroism, and tell with touching fidelity the price so many of our noble soldiers pay for their devotion to Queen and country; but other scenes there are which provide welcome comic relief, and arouse hearty laughter.
  – *Newcastle Chronicle* (c.1901)

Audiences were generally limited to stock footage of locations, occasional films from the front which were largely devoid of any representation of the conflict itself, and a raft of fake combat films. Audiences were rarely fooled, but nor were they left with a sense of being cheated by exhibitors, as contemporary reviews reveal. There was a common perception that fake or sham films abounded, as this typical article reveals:

Sham War Cinematograph Films – A correspondent asks us how he is to know real from sham war films, seeing that several subjects are made up at home from life models? The subject lends itself so well to life model work that one has to a great extent to rely on common sense: for instance in one film we have heard about, there is a hand-to-hand encounter between Boers and British, all realistic in its way, but the effect is somewhat spoilt by reason of the fringe of an audience appearing in the picture occasionally. Thus, when one sees gentlemen with tall hats, accompanied by ladies, apparently looking on, common sense would at once pronounce the film of the sham order. The same may be said of films showing soldiers lying and firing from behind 'earthworks', composed of nicely arranged straw. (Anon. 1900a, p.3)

The conceit was even celebrated in a popular music hall song:

Then the dizzling Kinetograph and its brave undaunted staff
Who've rented a secluded park not far from gay Paree;
Their methods, though dramatic, are a little bit erratic,
For they can't resist the joy of making British soldiers flee!
Their Khaki-covered camera is the latest thing,

As a fabrication-mill it is the greatest thing;
Two hundred lies a minute! Why, Kruger isn't in it
With this quite unanswerable film-beats-platest thing!
(Anon. 1900b: 300)

Despite the knowledge that what they were seeing was often a fake or reconstruction, audiences responded to these films as part of a much larger narrative of patriotic and nationalistic sentiment. This allowed the medium the license to deceive, and yet confirm a mass ideological position in support of the war. Audiences engaged in a knowing complicity with film-makers and exhibitors and used these texts in a sophisticated manner which relied heavily on the broader political context within which they were viewed.

The sophistication of audiences allowed film-makers to blend representations of 'real' people and situations with 'unreal' or fictional contexts. Audiences became adept at distinguishing between scenarios that had been elaborately staged for the benefit of the camera and films that depicted real events. Yet, the representations of the cinema which appeared in other media forms tended to portray it as an essentially realist medium. For example, it was often characterised as a medium ideally suited to uncovering the truth and to the detection and identification of individuals. Stories about people recognising missing relatives, or people pictured in compromising situations, became central to narratives representing cinema as an institution. The following extract from the World's Fair of 1909 is indicative of the prevalence of this type of story:

Tell-Tale Photograph: Wife's Deception Discovered at a Cinematograph Show — A man named Julian Boistard presented himself at the police station of Petit-Montrouge on Monday to give himself up for the murder of his wife. He had shot her with a revolver as the result of a quarrel, which arose in a curious way. Boistard had been to see a cinematograph display in the Rue de la Gaite, and among the pictures was one representing the Rheims aviation week. On the films he recognised his wife, making merry at the buffet. His wife, who was by his side, also recognised the tell-tale picture and fainted, whilst the wronged husband cried out his woes to the audience. He had believed his wife to be spending a holiday with some relations, while he was doing his military service. The performance was suspended, the lady taken to a chemist's and brought round. Then the couple went home, and the quarrel ensued. Fortunately for all concerned, the angry husband's aim was bad and he had not hit his wife at all. She had merely fainted again. He was set at liberty by the commissary on the understanding that the quarrel should be made up. (Anon. 1909a)

Fantasy, disengagement

The cinema, initially characterised as a medium best suited to representing reality, was also a site of spectatorial disengagement. The audience was presented with a world of fantastic and often disconcerting attractions. Film had the power to picture the impossible and improbable. It could arrest, reverse, slow or accelerate time; objects could be made to vanish, fly or change. Cinema offered bizarre perspectives, for example the 360° panoramic view, and manipulated its audience through a wide variety of technical trickery. Film-makers were immediately concerned with exploiting these particular characteristics of cinema, in absorbing particular conventions from existing popular spectacles and developing new and more fantastic applications. The stage and screen were well used to the representation of the fantastic and unusual. The traditions of magic, illusion and deception were centuries old, yet the novelty of the moving cinema-screen image, and its initial absorption into a competing market of attractions, occasioned a variety of responses.

One of the earliest responses was the demonstration of the particular facility of the medium to alter perceptions of real time. Audiences were well used to the conceits of narrative time shifts within literature and theatre, but were unprepared for real-time transformations. Exhibitors delighted audiences by affecting temporal changes through altering the speed of their projectors, or reversing the film and thus reversing time.

The tradition of illusions and visual trickery was also well established in a variety of sophisticated contexts, and these were replicated by many early practitioners such as Georges Méliès, Ferdinand Zecca and R. W. Paul. Méliès in particular was responsible for the development of the cinematic tradition of the trick film. He was originally proprietor of the Robert Houdin Magic Theatre in Paris and pioneered the adaptation of traditional theatrical illusions for the cine camera. The stage tradition, which relied on the use of trapdoors, false sets, gauzes, mirrors, lantern and lighting effects, was aided by editing and superimposition techniques to create astonishing illusions such as *The Man With The India-Rubber Head* (1902) and his most famous film, *Voyage to The Moon* (1902). R. W. Paul also developed the production of trick films and demonstrated another type of response to the illusory potential of cinema, conceiving of an entertainment which mixed cinema with other media to create a virtual reality machine. Others, such as the magician David Devant, had seen the potential for including cinema within other entertainments, but Paul's ideas, expressed in a magazine interview, took on a whole new dimension:

> He had been reading the weird romance, *The Time Machine*, and it had suggested an entertainment to him, of which animated photographs formed an essential part. In a room capable of accommodating some hundred people, he would arrange seats to which a slight motion could be given. He would plunge the apartment into Cimmerian darkness, and introduce a wailing wind. Although the audience actually moved but a few inches, the sensation would be of travelling through space. From time to time the journey would be combined with panoramic effects. Fantastic scenes of future ages would first be shown. Then the audience would set forth upon its homeward journey. The conductor would regretfully intimate that he had over-shot the mark, and travelled into the past – cue for another series of pictures. Mr Paul had for a long time been at work on this scheme, and had discussed it here and there. (Anon. 1896b)

Although Paul's time machine was never realised, other virtual entertainments were. Film-makers delighted in the presentation of seemingly impossible points of view. Cameras were taken up mountains, in hot air balloons, and attached to moving vehicles. Billy Bitzer strapped himself and his camera to the front of a speeding steam train to give the audience an engine-eye view. Film-makers originated what became known as the 'phantom ride' film, an enduring and often used genre. George Hale's 1904 entertainment at the St. Louis Fair, subsequently known as *Hale's Tours*, combined the cinematic and the dramatic. Audiences were seated within a replica railway carriage, complete with movement and smoke, and were presented with a cinematic tour of the world in the form of a global phantom ride projected in the windows of the carriage. Other entertainments, such as virtual big-game hunting, enjoyed brief popularity (Anon. 1909b). These attractions demonstrated not only the use of cinema as a means of disengagement from the audience's contemporary reality, but even began to offer a surrogate version of reality, making clear the potential of film as a kind of virtual reality apparatus.

Conclusion

In the years before 1914, the technology of moving pictures was adopted within multiple institutional contexts, ranging from political parties and pressure groups, to medical schools and religious societies. Its subsequent development as the premier entertainment medium of the first half of the twentieth century should not colour our historical understanding of a medium whose applications were the subject of extensive and often heated debate. Examining the primary uses of cinema allows us to interrogate the development of the medium, its evolution from scientific and entertainment novelty to dynamic worldwide institution within such a relatively short period of time. It also demonstrates the intertextual and intermedial nature of film, particularly in its ability to present a range of complex narratives to diverse, but increasingly visually literate, audiences.

4   EXHIBITION AND RECEPTION

Understanding early film spectatorship

For modern cinemagoers it is hard to imagine the experiences of early film audiences. Audiences were subject to a range of exhibition contexts and practices, some of which were centuries old, others emerging from the intrinsic potential of the new medium. In each country, at each type of entertainment site, from show to show, and even between performances of the same show, the style of delivery and the composition of the audience often changed radically. For example, in the UK, certain itinerant showmen interspersed their weekday performances on fairgrounds, which sometimes promised disreputable or salacious films, with Sunday 'sacred concerts' for the faithful (see Kember 2000). Clearly the range of films screened and the style of the showman involved underwent a dramatic transformation for the pious congregation (who perhaps had already visited the same show under different conditions!).

Throughout the industrialised world, cinema increasingly entered existing performance venues and traditions. For example, several – largely unsuccessful – attempts were made to incorporate the cinematograph into the legitimate theatre, where the moving picture was sometimes used as a moving backdrop to the action on stage.[1] Equally, on the other side of the entertainment spectrum, travelling showmen found that the novelty of the moving picture also had an enduring appeal to audiences.

In the years before 1910, cinematographs were regularly used in surprising combinations with other forms of sideshow entertainment. Moving pictures were introduced to entertainments from circuses and menageries, to magic shows, on each occasion supplementing the more traditional forms of entertainment associated with these sites. Even the Punch and Judy showman, 'Professor Stone', used a cinematograph in the open air during summer nights. 'The whole lot make a good strong show', he claimed of his marionette/cinematograph combination.[2] In each case, seasoned performers successfully adapted a traditional craft of performance in order to accommodate the increasingly popular novelty of moving pictures.

By 1900 the cinematograph was a pervasive feature within innumerable entertainment sites throughout European and American cities. Moving pictures could be viewed in lecture theatres and town halls, in vaudeville and variety theatres, in empty shops on busy thoroughfares, and even on street corners where street cinematograph 'peep-shows' proved a popular, if short-lived, attraction. Perhaps most important in bringing the phenomenon to universal prominence were the travelling showmen on the fairgrounds. In the UK, France, Australia, and Germany especially, but also in the US and numerous other countries, itinerant shows ensured that film reached a remarkably wide public long before provincial or rural audiences were easily able to travel to the city.

In the past twenty years, film historians have exploited a wide range of documentary sources in order to uncover the details of these disparate performance practices. In particular, national trade journals from the entertainment field, such as, in the UK, *The Era* (which carried news from variety and legitimate theatres), *The Optical Magic Lantern and Photographic Enlarger Journal* (lantern and lecturing news), *The World's Fair* (fairground news), *The Showman* (news for itinerant showmen), and *The Bioscope* (film news), besides many others, have become an invaluable resource. The occasional survival of anecdotes, memorabilia, and personal reminiscences of early film shows may also be useful in gauging the general trends and 'flavour' of early exhibitions. In the light of research conducted from such sources, local newspapers have offered much more specific, often critical, accounts of individual shows.

Research of this kind is painstaking and prolonged, and can resemble detective work as new resources are tracked down and identified, but the rewards are correspondingly substantial. Researchers are able to bring to light new and surprising details of film exhibition, altering our understanding of early audiences and therefore of the significance of the films themselves. In the past twenty years, studies of this kind have shown that early film exhibition was deeply implicated in heterogeneous nineteenth-century exhibition cultures. The trick has been to identify the initial contribution of early film to these cultures and to demonstrate how exhibitors and audiences were able to exploit the new medium in order to reproduce the traditional pleasures of the show. However, as new sources are uncovered and new approaches taken to the early film audience, it is vital to remember that the first people to address such questions were early film-makers and exhibitors. Indeed, several films were dedicated to the theme of film spectatorship, borrowing directly from a sub-genre of comic and trick film-making in which the activities of on-screen audiences became the focus of the comedy. For example, Robert Paul's *The Countryman and the Cinematograph* (1901) shows the naïve reactions of a country yokel to a series of films, including his terror at the approach of a train on-screen. The joke at the expense of the terrified rube was popular enough to be filmed again (or 'duped' as this practice was called) by American Bioscope under the title, *Uncle Josh at the Moving Picture Show* (1902). British film-maker George Albert Smith had already gone one step further in his *Snapshotting an Audience* (1900) by offering audiences an image of another audience staring directly back at them and also misbehaving to comic effect. These films gave spectators a reflection of their own viewing strategies, demonstrating that excessive naïveté or misbehaviour during the show were to be ridiculed and rejected by the accomplished spectator.

In the Pathé Cinematograph Company catalogue for May 1903, nestled amongst a series of short comic and magic trick films, a film appears that warrants close attention. As its title suggests, *A Cinematograph Show* gave spectators of the cinematograph a bizarre reflection of the conditions of their own spectatorship. The film itself does not survive;

all that remains is a single frame accompanied by a simple description within the catalogue:

Here we are present at a genuine Cinematograph show, reproduced by the Cinematograph, and we see successively 6 different subjects. The interest of the scene, is still increased, owing to the fact, that the statues in the frame, the boxers, the public and the operator himself are all the same person, viz: one person plays as many as 8 different parts at the same time.[3]

What use can we make of this sparse information? At first glance, even this brief description appears to present students of early film with a series of conundrums. Let us imagine how it might have played out for actual audiences. In the course of an actual film show, the exhibition of A Cinematograph Show – at 160 feet lasting approximately 90 seconds – would have appeared as one element of a much more extensive programme. During this film, a second screen was represented within the frame of the real screen. Upon the second screen, a series of six films, including a boxing scene, was played to an on-screen audience. In the meantime, statues on either side of the second screen came magically to life, and members of the on-screen audience, including the on-screen cinematograph operator, turned to the camera to address the real audience. And at the heart of this bewildering array of looks between real and on-screen audiences, operators and performers came the absurd revelation that every character on screen, including performers, spectators, animated statues and operators, was in fact played by the same person! How were contemporary audiences able to interpret this moving picture? More importantly, for modern students of early cinema, how can we begin to answer this question when the film at issue has become all but indecipherable to us?

The key to interpreting this film must begin with an understanding of its original audience and the possible contexts of its exhibition. For an audience of 1903, the film probably held few surprises. For modern historians, A Cinematograph Show offers a number of coded reflections on the practices early cinema audiences. Above all, the film demonstrates the heterogeneity of the early film experience. It emphasises that spectators responded not to one style of performance, but to many, not only to the performers on the screen, but also to those on the stage beneath it and even to the cinematograph operator standing within the auditorium. A series of layered live performances, with the film itself at their centre, all played a substantial and visible role in entertaining audiences.

Furthermore, in addition to the heterogeneity of layered performances and performance styles the film also reflects upon the mechanism that enabled spectators to make sense of all this. In particular, the replication of the same face playing all of these different roles suggests the enduring significance of personality to the successful film institution. In an era when audiences were becoming increasingly accustomed to watching performances that had been recorded at another time and in another place, the film demonstrates that the gap between the performers and audiences was not as great as it seemed. The personal appeal of a showman could speak volumes to audiences long used to the tradition of showmanship, who were perhaps still uncertain or distrustful of the new medium of film.[4]

In this light, far from presenting an insoluble conundrum, *A Cinematograph Show* represents a remarkably cogent response to the demands of exhibitors and audiences in 1903. The film may be seen as a response to an early audience who were intimately concerned with the novelty of film exhibition and spectatorship, but whose understanding of films was largely dependent upon a range of more familiar and traditional attractions, such as the exhibition of scientific novelties, magic and illusion. Equally important were the venues within which these attractions were staged.

Pre-cinematic traditions: science and magic

The first exhibitions of film were often made to scientific institutions, for whom the moving picture represented an advance upon pre-existing optical and chemical technologies, particularly photography and chronophotography. Scientific technologies were commonly exhibited as entertainment in a variety of venues. Throughout the nineteenth century, popular science lectures had become a common feature of most performance venues, with famous figures making regular appearances on the podium. The popularity of these events increasingly brought scientific discovery into the realm of popular culture. By the turn of the century, demonstrations of electricity and other scientific phenomena proved major attractions and were often combined with other entertainments such as magic and illusion. These scientific novelties were commonly presented by magicians as part of their show, as well as other popular pseudo-sciences such as mesmerism and mind-reading. One particular venue, the Egyptian Hall in London, became especially associated with this kind of performance and was popularly known as 'England's Home of Mystery'. Located in Piccadilly alongside several other popular Victorian attractions, the Egyptian Hall contained two exhibition spaces, and its façade had been modelled after the Temple of Osiris in order to reflect the contemporary vogue for Egyptology and oriental mysticism. From 1873, Neville Maskelyne and Alfred Cooke presented magic shows at the Hall, and their brand name, 'Maskelyne & Cooke', became synonymous with illusionism and sleight of hand. In the next thirty years, their key attractions included the magician David Devant and some of the earliest film performances in the UK. Georges Méliès and Robert W. Paul were frequent visitors, Paul supplying Devant with a Theatrograph projector, which he incorporated into his magic show. Devant also appeared in one of Paul's earliest films, entitled *Maskelyne: Spinning Plates* (1896).

By 1901, the show included a succession of performances and was widely celebrated in the popular and trade press. We now include the first half of a lengthy review in order to demonstrate the scale, variety and sophistication of this integrated performance, within which films played an important role:

At England's Home of Mystery WHO has not heard of the Egyptian Hall, and of the miracles performed by that famous old wizard, Mr. J. A Maskelyne? The fame of the establishment and its proprietor has spread to every corner of the globe, and there is no visitor to our City of London who does not pay at least one visit to this quaint old building.

Mr. Maskelyne knows his patrons, and the visitors know their entertainer; everybody is comfortable, and there is a kind of reciprocal good feeling between the actors and the audience; indeed, we know of no other place or amusement where such a state of all-round content exists. Accustomed as its patrons are to programmes of the best, Mr. Maskelyne has made his present entertainment fairly shine with the brilliancy of first-class talent. That his efforts are appreciated is very evident by the crowded houses that witness every performance; and on the afternoon of our visit, the place was packed, excepting the seats which the management had kindly reserved for ourselves.

Part One of the programme consists of an exhibition of pure sleight-of-hand by Herr Valadon, who, in deference to the wishes of the audience, has revived his coin manipulation experiments and the miser's dream; after which he gives a demonstration of card palming, and concludes his first appearance on the programme with a rising card trick. Altogether, this first item forms a very palatable dish, and proves the artiste's ability as a dextrous exponent of the art. The hall then darkens for the animated photographs, and, would you believe it, they are simply known by that plain title. Mr. Maskelyne introduces the pictures, explaining their various phases as they move along, and occasionally pointing out some celebrity who might have otherwise escaped our notice. Luckily, visitors are not bored by too much of one subject, and the management are by no means conservative in their ideas, for they present quite as many comical films as those of historical and momentary interest. The slight delay in adjusting the films and changing the spools is admirably occupied by Mr. C. W. Locke with a series of trinoptic lantern effects. These views are most beautiful, and the changes from day to night are strikingly realistic. During the projection of the pictures and views, Mr. F. Cramer accompanies them with suitable selections upon Mr. Maskelyne's mechanical orchestra.

Then Herr & Madam Valadon present a collection of psychological problems that are really astounding. Granting that the experiments are the outcome of scientific trickery, we must give the performers every credit for possessing such abnormal memories, and for being endowed with a quickness of perception far above the general average.

Herr Valadon thoroughly explains the nature of the performance before commencing, so that it will not be necessary for him to speak again until the experiments are concluded; and then the lady is blind-folded.

Two blackboards are upon the stage, one of which is plain, while the other is squared up and numbered in the form of a chess-board. A pack of cards is handed to be shuffled, and two independent gentlemen in the audience each take a hand for a game at nap. Another gentleman is requested to write down an addition sum of four lines of four figures, and someone else is asked to call out the number of any square upon which to commence the difficult chess problem known as 'The Knight Gambit.'

Madam now commences, and she never hesitates for one moment; away she skips over the chess-board, carrying the knight some dozen or so legitimate moves, before she suddenly instructs the gentleman in the audience upon her right that he will call and get three tricks on his hand, and that the gentleman upon her left will allow his opponent to play. Under her direction, both gentlemen play the cards she names, with the result that the caller scores the first trick. Then the lady starts upon the addition sum, and tells the figure that is to be put under the column of units, and then on to the chess-board again. Picking the knight's tour up from where it was let drop, Madam Valadon sends it on its course again, soon branching off into the game of cards, and from there on to the addition sum. At last the Knight Gambit has been successfully accomplished, and the last card has been played, winning three tricks for the gentleman she named. The addition sum is then brilliantly finished, and Madam bows to the applause. Every clap is fully earned, for her triple experiment has been accomplished; and be it remembered that not one word is spoken during the whole business – it is prodigious!

Part II now makes its bow.[5]

The article takes us through each stage of the entertainment, describing in turn the sleight-of-hand performances of Herr Valadon; the films presented by Neville Maskelyne – the proprietor of the Hall; and a series of feats of memory conducted by Herr and Madam Valadon. In part two, a lengthy sketch entitled *The Entranced Fakir* was performed, in which a series of illusionist tricks were incorporated into a simple storyline. Thus, we can see that the films were co-ordinated with a range of other performances, even during screening.

The performance was accompanied by Maskelyne's commentary on the films and the 'mechanical orchestra', confirming that the tendency to regard early cinema as a silent spectacle is false. Evidence suggests that the traditions of pre-cinema performance, such as the use of a lecturer, musical accompaniment, sound effects and audience reactions informed cinema performance, providing a complex and sophisticated auditory accompaniment to the image track (see Abel & Altman 2001). This was subsequently replaced or supplemented by new technologies for recording synchronous images and sound, such as Leon Gaumont's Chronophone apparatus.

From beginning to end, the show bombarded spectators with a sequence of attractions in very much the manner described by Gunning's model of the cinema of attractions. However, even at the Egyptian Hall, the review gives us good reason to suppose that the dynamic of shock and disquiet remained secondary to a more conventional form of address most strongly associated with the longstanding nineteenth century tradition of magic and illusionist shows. The article reinforces the contribution of Neville Maskelyne to his own show on several occasions, and conveys a strong sense of comfort and familiarity between performer and audience. 'Mr. Maskelyne knows his patrons', confirms the reviewer, 'and the visitors know their entertainer; everybody is comfortable, and there is a kind of reciprocal good feeling between the actors and the audience'. In this context, Maskelyne's role as lecturer of the films is especially significant, marking his ownership not only of the exhibition site and the show, but also of the delivery of the entertainment and the responses of his audiences. The show at the Egyptian Hall inherited much of its content and style from an earlier institution of conjuring performance, and it is not surprising that much of the appeal of the show rested upon a surprisingly intimate relationship between the conjuror and his audience.

Early film shows of all kinds often depended on the live performances of a number of showmen for their success. Furthermore, acknowledging the variety of these earlier performance traditions enables us to understand the variety of ways in which they could be exploited by individual institutions. In this light, the primary lesson to be learned from this review is that different traditions of live performance, drawn from the conjuring show, the illusionist spectacle, the magic lantern show, the educational lecture and even the popular and legitimate theatres, might be exploited by a single institution for the benefit of its audiences. The screening of early films merely reflected upon these traditions and, in this case, represents another influence upon the long evolution of performance strategies at the Egyptian Hall.

This multiple performance characterised the exhibition strategies which developed in a variety of venues. This is particularly evident in early traditions of film exhibition that pre-date the emergence of the picture theatre. In the UK, exhibitors made use of a variety of performance contexts from the church hall to the fairground, from the street corner to music hall. The following two case studies explore the use made of these venues by individual showmen and demonstrate the techniques they used to satisfy widely varying audiences at each site.

The itinerant exhibitor: William Slade

William Slade was a well established shoe seller from Cheltenham, holder of a Royal Warrant, and part-time magic lanternist. Accompanied by his daughter Mary, and in partnership with a theatrical and music hall agent

Edward Barring, Slade toured Britain between May 1897 and March 1898. In this period of little under a year he and his daughter gave up to three lantern and film shows a day in over 190 locations including theatres, music halls, church halls, a minor English public school and two Royal Navy warships, HMS Bascowen and HMS Minotaur. The basis of Slade's career as a film exhibitor was obviously motivated by the financial rewards associated with cinema and backed by his experiences as an amateur lanternist.

The trade press was full of accounts of fortunes to be made exhibiting films, reviews of the latest technology and practical advice relating to exhibition – to which as a magic lanternist he would have been exposed. For example, Edmund Robins published an article entitled 'Hints on Exhibiting Cinematographs' prefaced thus:

> The cinematograph is now becoming such an important part of all public entertainments, that a few words upon the management of a show may not be entirely out of place, coming as they do from experience gained while on tour in the provinces with one of these instruments. (Robins 1897)

And *The Photographic Dealer,* in an article entitled 'How Dealers Make Money Out Of Kinematographs', in the same month that year, hinted not only at the stability of audiences, but at the money to be made in the regions:

> Kinematograph shows are patronised as well as ever, and the audiences are just as enthusiastic as those of 12 months ago, in spite of the number of entertainments of this kind which are now in full swing. In smaller towns and country districts where the machines have not yet penetrated the dealer has the whole field to himself. (Anon. 1897)

The possibilities for regional success were certainly attractive enough for William Slade to abandon a respectable high street business for over a year and embark with his daughter on a highly speculative enterprise. The

Advertising postcard for Arthur Elvy and Raymond's Bioscope (1906) demonstrating the mixed variety performance.

performances not only had to sustain Slade and his daughter but also turn enough profit to provide a dividend for their partner Edward Barring, account for all expenses relating to the performances, which were considerable, and provide the substantial initial capital for equipment and films.

Slade embarked on two distinct tours: the first a series of twenty dates between May and June 1897, culminating in a two-day engagement at the Winter Gardens in his home town of Cheltenham to celebrate Queen Victoria's Diamond Jubilee. These two days were devoid of films of the Jubilee – but the Jubilee was to be at the heart of Slade's subsequent tour and his partnership with Edward Barring. The second tour was initially to last 8 weeks but eventually ran to 28, with 170 separate dates. It began in the southwest, passing through Devon and Cornwall, then to the north covering Lincolnshire and Yorkshire, Lancashire and the Lake District, finishing in Scotland.

For almost nine months Slade and his daughter exhibited Jubilee films, lantern views and a changing roster of music hall performers. The contract between Slade and Barring made very clear the responsibilities of both parties: Slade was responsible for the films and equipment, Barring the organisation and booking of venues and supplementary artistes. The tour made full use of two distinctive types of venue exploited by itinerant shows: the popular theatre and municipal exhibition venues.

Slade's tour was primarily based on the well-established music hall circuits. In the music hall, as in vaudeville in the US, cinema was part of a competing bill of variety attractions. These were located in large towns and cities and were usually seen as secondary venues in relation to the legitimate theatre. As in the Egyptian Hall, a succession of performances would take place on the variety theatre stage and existed in competition with other acts, including comedians, musical interludes, acrobats, dramatic sketches, and magicians. Films were often used as part of these acts, sometimes even providing a backdrop to dramatic sequences. However, they also appeared independently, particularly in reaction to major news events such as the Boer War, where they provided a form of news service and a focus for popular patriotism. Initially, films were a remarkable novelty attraction on the music hall circuit, sometimes topping the bill of attractions in preference to established music hall stars. However, the cinema quickly became a conventional attraction in the Halls, appearing as a support to big name acts such as the comedians Dan Leno and Herbert Campbell.

Slade's performances also took place in a variety of other public spaces, such as town halls, lecture theatres, and church halls. Within these municipal venues, which tended to attract different types of audience, a different performance style predominated, often drawing heavily upon the format of magic lantern lectures and offering moral guidance and religious education. As the lecturer spoke, still or moving images served to illustrate the points raised, or were used to punctuate the lecture at key points. For example, the tradition of the temperance lecture, in which audiences were shown the evils of drink, were a common feature of such venues. Lecturing societies, which invited professional visiting lecturers to speak about their subjects of expertise, also embraced the arrival of the moving picture. By the turn of the century, however, professional lecturers were increasingly in competition with moving pictures, which were beginning to tell purely visual stories far more effectively.

The showman: Tom Norman

Tom Norman, our second example, was a professional British showman, whose career spanned at least four decades from the 1870s and took him from freak shows to cinematograph shows to the auction room. Unlike Slade, he was primarily associated with the fairground Bioscope show and street cinema in the form of the penny gaff. He therefore offers us a good example of film exhibition at these important, largely working-class, venues. For Norman, the moving picture promised a new novelty to add to his already impressive roster of novelties, freaks and other 'Living Wonders'. It gave the showman another opportunity to entice paying customers into the show, where their spectatorship was often noisy and confrontational.

The invaluable surviving manuscript of Norman's own *Memoirs* can give us an intriguing, if suspiciously exaggerated, glimpse into the

Advertisement for Tom Norman's Freak Shows (*The Era Almanack*, December 1893).

practices of showland culture at the turn of the nineteenth century, and we must be circumspect in our interpretation of such material.[6] These memoirs concentrate upon his 'shop-front shows', often called penny gaffs, at the turn of the century. These were small shops, usually rented on busy thoroughfares, in which it was possible to exhibit any marketable novelty or curiosity. Indeed, Norman boasted that in hard times he would 'exhibit any mortal thing for money ... no matter how repulsive, or how demoralising' (Norman n.d.: 26). This is what Norman had to say about his chain of shop-front cinematograph shows:

> But you could indeed exhibit anything in those days, yes anything
> from a needle to an anchor, a flea to an elephant, a bloater, you

could exhibit as a whale. It was not the show, it was the tale that you told.

The public had no where else to go.

There was very few music halls outside of London, No two houses a night places, and Picture Palaces, well they were not thought of.

Speaking of moving pictures, I remember that when they were first exhibited, that I had at the time, three shops in Chrisp Street Poplar, all small places, but I engaged a Bioscope as we termed it to open in one of the above places.

The operator fixed his machine just inside of the entrance, leaving only sufficient room for the audience to get in and out.

There was no fixed time of commencing, the performance started when the place was full of people.

Sometimes we had a house full of people, and the cylinders of gas what was used for the light in the projector had not arrived.

I would then have to send one of my men inside to give a comic song, and keep the people entertained whilst waiting for the gas to turn up. (Norman n.d.: 13)

Norman dwells on the central importance of the showman to the successful moving picture entertainment and repeats a belief regularly expressed at the time that the good show depended upon the showman's ingenuity under unfavourable circumstances. Furthermore, the manuscript speaks of the cinematograph as merely another novelty in a showland culture that had long exploited the novelty of freaks and curiosities. In fact, these descriptions strongly resemble the few other surviving accounts of penny gaff cinematograph shows.[7] Sometimes, the performances recorded on nitrate were less significant during the show than those live performances recorded only in the occasional anecdote or memoir.

Norman also owned and ran shows on the fairground, including Bioscope shows. The fairground Bioscope was arguably the most important exhibition site before the establishment of purpose-built cinemas, and was certainly responsible for introducing film entertainments to rural populations. The English fair had long traditions in terms of venue, reappearing at the same sites regularly each year. They were not only sites of entertainment but had also served important economic functions; they were often the location at which labourers and domestic staff could be hired and livestock traded. The fairs were largely closed to outsiders, and membership and status within the organisation depended on family connections. By the turn of the century, fairs in the UK usually centred around one or more roundabouts, with many other rides and shows surrounding them.

Walking through the fairground, audiences were actively solicited on all sides by showmen, known as 'barkers', who would tout for their business, inviting them to enter their show. First introduced to the fairground in 1896 by showman Randall Williams, the Bioscope shows became a dominant presence in most fairs until 1914. Indeed, in many fairs they had replaced more traditional entertainments and could often be found lined up in a row, offering alternative programmes of films to audiences. At every stage of the Bioscope show spectators were confronted with a series of familiar showman-led attractions. The show fronts were beautifully adorned, often including a fairground organ and a small stage upon which eye-catching variety performers known as 'paraders' would perform alongside the barkers. Tempted to pay their pennies, the customers would enter, carefully marshalled by the 'step men', into the main exhibition space. This was a large tented structure sometimes containing over a thousand comfortable seats. Within, customers could expect a wide variety of films, from factual representations of Boer War scenes, to comic representations of variety performers and salacious depictions of erotic dances. Alongside these screen attractions, audiences could expect live musical performances, magic lantern lectures, further entertainments by the paraders and the presence of a film 'describer', as he was known, who would interpret the action on-screen for the benefit of patrons.

In common with other mixed entertainment venues, the fairground Bioscope gradually became obsolete, being increasingly replaced by static purpose-built picture houses, which began a process of standardisation and regularisation of cinema exhibition.

Advertisement for the Warwick Trading Company illustrating the parade of a fairground show (*The Showman*, 22 November 1901).

Electric theatres and picture houses

In the years after 1908, in most countries, historians agree that a decisive shift took place within the developing film industry. In particular, a movement towards more consistent forms of film spectatorship was typified by the development of the new 'Electric Theatres' and 'Picture Palaces'. The rapid development of grandiose purpose-built movie houses ensured that live performances, which easily became repetitive for local audiences, were supplanted by performances on-screen, which could be varied dramatically by merely changing the film reel. The new theatres favoured longer programmes, longer films, and encouraged audiences to return each week and watch a new programme from beginning to end (Hiley 1998: 96–103). The aggressive spread of electric theatre chains throughout the US and Europe was an indication of this consolidation of patterns of spectatorship. Reinforced in many countries by the development of safety legislation prejudicial to earlier sites of exhibition, the years of the creative exhibitor gradually came to an end.

In this changing environment, traces of earlier modes of performance survived for a surprisingly long period. The performance of film lecturers has been recorded in various countries as late as the 1920s and 1930s. Arguably the role of cinema managers in promoting forthcoming attractions to audiences preserved an attenuated form of the showman's patter. However, catalogues increasingly offered self-enclosed fictional films to exhibitors that did not depend on live performance at the exhibition site. These were now rented to their customers on short lease so that the efficient circulation of film attractions could be easily maintained. Lecturing itself ultimately retreated from its traditional role during exhibition to become part of the sales patter of distributors: 'While the original purpose of lectures is almost extinct', wrote the American David S. Hulfish in 1915, 'their advertising value remains and they are used by manufacturers in large quantities' (Hulfish 1915: 112). The lecture's move backwards from exhibition to production and distribution reflected the growing importance of institutions of production and the decline of institutions of exhibition in their influence over spectatorship. Some showmen followed the lecture and entered the film business as screenwriters or producers. Others opted for invisibility and opened their own chains of static picture theatres during the 1910s.

The new exhibition strategy of the picture palaces depended intimately upon a parallel development in film form. In particular, patterns of film exhibition and spectatorship were now closely regulated by the pleasures afforded by a good story. In tracing the development of narrative film, the film student is therefore obliged to consider the characteristic opportunities it offered to exhibitors and the pleasures it offered to audiences.

In Britain, by 1914, the actual experience of going to the cinema varied from city to city, town to town and cinema to cinema. Cinemas ranged from modest 100–200 seaters in converted halls to purpose-built 2,000 luxury seaters in London and the larger provincial cities, with potted palms, cafes and cloakrooms. They were still often regarded as rather unsavoury places, and in a handbook for managers published in 1912 advice was given on how to disinfect the cinema with the audience in occupation (see Harding & Popple 1996: 229). An advert from the Walturdaw Company Catalogue of 1911 pays testimony to the benefits of such practices:

Those proprietors of Theatres, Picture Palaces, Music, Concert and Dancing Halls, who have adopted the system of the 'Perolin' Air Purification are unanimous in praise of it, and this is endorsed by their audiences who know how to appreciate the cool and fragrant wave of freshness and humidity in the crowded foyer or heated auditorium. (Anon. 1911)

It has been estimated that by 1914 there were between 5,000–7,000 cinemas in Britain and around 75,000 people were employed at all levels within the industry.[8] London alone – including the suburbs – had 600, Manchester 111 and Liverpool 33. The average projectionist's wage was 35s a week and roughly equal to that of a pianist, the usual accompaniest to silent films. Larger cinemas employed trios or quartets, and the largest concert orchestras. Whatever the status of the establishment, there was usually some form of aural accompaniment for the films being exhibited, whether in the person of a narrator or film explainer, added sound effects, music, or synchronised cylinder or disc recordings.

Admission naturally varied depending on the status of the cinema and the films being screened, but on average ranged between 3d and 1s 3d a seat. Films were changed bi-weekly and a typical mixed programme of films lasted between one to two hours, and generally ran continuously. Film was often rented by length, so much for a foot, rather than by any qualitative judgement. The overwhelming majority of films seen by British audiences were foreign, usually American or continental. They were often rented on exclusive terms to major cinemas or chains of cinemas. The average rental for a first feature programme was £24 per week in 1914, £16 for a second feature, whereas the tendency in 1896 was to purchase films outright, with films often in circulation for many months, even years, as they ran down the scale of regional venues.

Conclusion

The period between 1896 and 1914 was characterised by rapid developments in film exhibition. Initially housed within a variety of pre-existing exhibition contexts, and part of disparate traditions of showmanship and performance, cinemas emerged as institutions in their own right, standardising all aspects of performance and focusing attention far more directly on the films themselves. Consequently, the way in which audiences viewed films altered perceptibly, as new visual storytelling strategies evolved. It is to these developments in film form that we now turn.

5   FILM FORM: GENRE AND NARRATIVE

Imagine, for a moment, that the year is 1900 and you are about to see your first moving picture. What do you expect to see? How might you begin to interpret the images flickering upon the screen?

Movies have become such a familiar part of our lives in the past century that such questions have become difficult to answer. We all have an implicit knowledge of the sophisticated conventions of storytelling and genre that have long been at the heart of the popular cinema, but this familiarity can also make it difficult to resurrect the responses of the earliest audiences to moving pictures. For these audiences an entirely different set of conventions was in play. We may attempt to recover this through an understanding of varied intertextual and intermedial influences on early cinema (see Kember 2001).

This chapter will introduce further strands of academic research that have contributed to our understanding of early cinema, but will concentrate especially upon the form and content of the films themselves. In part, this raises well-rehearsed questions concerned with the formal properties of early film texts and especially with the early development of story films. In recent years, however, revisionist historians have demonstrated that this development was only one element in a much more sophisticated transition. More than any other medium, early films exemplify the transition from the disparate entertainment traditions of the nineteenth century to the centralised mass media culture of the twentieth. Unlike live performances in the theatre or the music hall, the recordings made possible by moving picture apparatus might be taken at any time and could be duplicated and distributed all over the world. However, although increasingly centralised, early film production was also characterised by a sophisticated system of genre classification that borrowed much from traditional entertainments. From the beginning, moving picture genres sought to reproduce tried and tested public attractions. It is to these attractions and to their inheritance in early cinema that we first turn.

Genre and tradition

Genre can be defined as a way of categorising texts according to their structure, style and content. Throughout the history of cinema, it has enabled film producers to differentiate their product and has helped audiences to select the films that interest them most. The success of any one genre is therefore closely tied to the requirements of film-makers and audiences and reflects upon the media culture and the broader society of which it is a part. A similar, but much more vigorous, process of genre definition took place in the first years of cinema.

As the novelty of moving pictures began to fade and the apparatus began to realise its full potential as a recording device, early film catalogues advertised ever more sophisticated genre distinctions to exhibitors. By 1897 film-makers, in the organisation of their catalogues, and exhibitors, in their film programmes, already distinguished between subjects such as 'general views', 'comic views' or 'travel views' for the benefit of their customers.

By 1903, the preferences of exhibitors and audiences had become rarefied and differentiated to such an extent that Cecil Hepworth's Hepwix company, among others, published a sophisticated 'Classified Index of Film Subjects' with its catalogue, enabling customers to skip directly to comic sub-genres such as 'Animated Portraits', 'Fire Scenes', 'Jokes on Policemen' or 'Reversing Films', if they so wished (Hepwix Catalogue 1903: 3–5).

Often these genres were reformulations for the screen of earlier entertainments and thus tended to depend on a range of attractions long familiar to their audiences. For example, the 1898 film *Will Evans, the Musical Eccentric* (Warwick Trading Company) represented the acrobatic tumbles and pratfalls of this well-known music hall performer. It was most likely screened within music halls and depended on the familiarity of their audiences with this kind of comedy 'turn', or even on the recognition of Will Evans himself. Similarly, films such as *Upside Down; or, The Human Flies* (Robert Paul, 1899) or *The Magician* (Thomas Edison 1900), in which a conjuror was depicted on-screen performing tricks, depended upon the familiarity of audiences with a nineteenth-century tradition of magic shows characterised by qualities of spectacle, surprise and sleight of hand.

In fact, these 'trick films' depended upon the development of clever special effects rather than upon the skill of the conjuror. In *The Human Flies*, the on-screen conjuror 'magically' makes four observers jump onto the ceiling where they walk around: an effect created by a hidden 'trick cut' between the two shots in which the room and all its furniture was inverted. A similar effect is achieved in *The Magician*, where a conjuror 'magically' causes a series of items to appear and disappear.

The cinematograph achieved a confounding mastery over space and time comparable to the work of the conjuror, and in trick films such as *Upside Down* or *The Magician* the conjuror himself was present, as if to justify the impossible action. However, even where he was not present, the magic show represented a primary frame for understanding the marvels of moving pictures. How was the illusion of moving pictures achieved? Who was responsible for it? Such questions were at the heart of many early film entertainments. More generally, as Michael Chanan has suggested, the conjuror was always a pertinent presence in early cinema: an inscrutable figure responsible for the miraculous reproduction of the world for spatially and temporally distant audiences (Chanan 1996: 117–22).

Other early cinema genres capitalised on this capacity of the cinematograph, like the photographic camera before it, to travel anywhere and record anything, from 'portraits' of famous people to street scenes of great cities, or panoramas of foreign landscapes. Indeed, for one writer in 1902, such films represented the future of the moving picture:

In the past, animated picture entertainments have mainly consisted in scenes of busy streets, bunkum conjuring, exhilarating experiences on the foot-plates of electric trams and railway trains, etc. In the future, we may look for further development of this interesting business. Already we are about to participate in the luxury of having all the topical incidents of the day illustrated and cartooned on the sheet at one of our London halls, but of that, more anon. The latest is the promise of a kind of trip round the world in an arm chair. A photographer has been despatched from London, with the necessary instructions, to Egypt, for the purpose of obtaining a continuous series of scenes on the way from Cairo to Khartoum. One thousand miles of the journey will be made by water, and the remainder by train or by such other means as may be found necessary. In the coming summer, the idea will be further extended, when picturesque portions of Canada will be photographed. (*The Showman*, 17 January 1902: 293)

The idea of 'armchair travel', here seen as a progressive alternative to the low-brow film genres that dominated the marketplace in 1902, had long been exploited across the entertainment spectrum in the UK. The popular early cinema genre of travel and picturesque subjects, which by 1902 had taken the camera to the top of Mont Blanc (*An Ascent of Mont Blanc, 15,781 feet high* [Warwick Trading Company]), and by 1912 to the heart of the Antarctic (*With Captain Scott to the South Pole* [Gaumont]), was closely related to a nineteenth-century tradition known as the 'travelogue' entertainment (see Kember 2003). Within travelogues, a lecturer would recount his adventures within foreign lands in a manner intended to impart both education and amusement to audiences. In the last decades of the nineteenth century these entertainments had usually been supplemented by the screening of appropriate magic lantern images for audiences, and to a limited extent the projection of illustrative moving images was seen as a natural step forward for the tradition. Travelling lantern lecturers like Henry Hibbert, who toured his Boer War entertainment in the UK from February 1900 and his popular lecture on

Paris in the spring of 1901, soon introduced films to their entertainments, either as interludes between sequences of slides, or as episodes worthy of commentary in themselves (*The Showman*, 22 March 1901: 168; *The Showman*, 12 April 1901). Famous American travelogue lecturer Burton Holmes' performances in British churches and lecture theatres in 1905 were especially celebrated by the *Optical Lantern and Cinematograph Journal*, which also took this rare opportunity to make a rallying call to lantern lecturers:

> In his description of the scenes there is nothing pretentious; no hard and dry-as-dust lecture, but a calm and interesting statement of facts which appeal to the audience, and give them a ready grasp of the subject and a large interest in the views portrayed. We have time after time advocated moving picture lectures, and if Mr. Holmes' Travelogues are taken as a pattern, the revival of the optical lantern would quickly be at hand. (*The Optical Lantern and Cinematograph Journal*, September 1905: 170)

For this writer, the travelogue represented an opportunity for lantern lecturers, who elsewhere bemoaned the sudden ascendancy of moving pictures over their own elocutionary performances, to capitalise on moving pictures. In fact, the travelogue film entertainment survived well into the 1910s and beyond in the UK, where it became an occasional attraction at those picture theatres which could guarantee an audience for this type of show and this genre of film. Arguably, the travel genre remains powerfully influential within the documentary film-making tradition today. However, dominant late nineteenth-century traditions such as the magic lantern show had a much more pervasive, if subtle, impact upon early film genres than this kind of gradual commercial transition immediately suggests. We now present two case studies of films, derived from pantomime and magic lantern traditions respectively, to chart this impact upon specific examples of early genre cinema.

Case study 1: Herbert Campbell as 'Little Bobbie' (British Mutoscope and Biograph Company, 1899)

Our first case study poses a potential puzzle for film historians and archivists. Only one copy of the film has survived, in the form of a Kinora Reel – a portable device produced by the British Mutoscope and Biograph Company that enabled people to view brief moving pictures in their own homes. The original title of the film is unknown, and its action, lasting less than a minute, seems so simple as to defy interpretation (see Kember 2001). In the course of the film, an enormously fat man wearing a bib sits centre-frame, a table in front of him. Gazing glassy-eyed at the camera he then proceeds messily to shovel a plateful of unidentifiable mush into his mouth, washing it down greedily with a bottle of beer. After a few seconds he has cleaned the plate and emptied the bottle (though much of it has spilled back out of his mouth and onto the table), and the man settles back in the chair with a grin conveying deep satisfaction.

What was the purpose of this grotesque little film? How might contemporary audiences have interpreted it? The answers to such questions lie in a careful exploration of earlier performance traditions and an understanding of early cinema genres.

Clearly, the British Biograph and Mutoscope Company considered the film's subject popular enough for retail to home audiences in the form of the Kinora reel.[1] As the provisional title, *Herbert Campbell as Little Bobbie*, suggests, the film brought the attractions of a well-known public personality to these disparate audiences. Like Will Evans, Herbert Campbell was a famous British star of the music hall at the turn of the nineteenth century. Throughout the year he would perform a variety of comedy 'star turns' in the Halls, but during the Christmas season he was especially associated with pantomime. The film is thought to represent a brief reprisal of his role as Little Bobbie in the 1899 Drury Lane theatre pantomime *Jack and the Beanstalk*. In fact, there is no comparable scene in the surviving text of this pantomime, and Little Bobbie actually directed his gluttonous attention only to pantomime prop food.[2] A surviving postcard of Little Bobbie also shows that Campbell is dressed rather differently. Therefore, it remains uncertain which of Campbell's characters is reproduced here, but there is a wealth of 'fat boy' personae to choose from: he was famously involved with the tradition of the comic pantomime feast every year at Drury Lane. This film represents for audiences at home the crowning moment of that feast, as Campbell wolfed his food with grotesque and comedic abandon.

Although interpretation of this film related specifically to the recognition of a music hall star, a brief survey of similar British productions in the years before 1903 reveals that the film was also part of a much broader comedy tradition, which subsequently led to the development of an early film genre popularly described as 'facials' in the trade catalogues.[3] These films presented the spectacle of a facial close-up, projected to a monstrous size on the screen, to audiences. The facial genre depended upon the virtuoso display of facial expressions. The genre proved sporadically popular in the US, UK and France between about 1897 and 1907. At the height of their popularity in the UK, the 1902 Warwick Trading Company catalogue listed some 33 entries in a separate 'Facial Expressions' section (Warwick Catalogue 1902: 9–10). Sometimes the performer would simply grimace and pull faces into the camera for no apparent reason, but mostly there was some simple narrative justification for this unusual display. For example, in *Facial Expressions: The Fateful Letter* (British Mutoscope and Biograph Company, 1898), performer Ben Nathan reads a letter – supposedly informing him that he is a beneficiary of his Aunt's will – with overblown expressions of concern, grief, astonishment, and happiness in swift succession. His eyes boggle and his mouth opens and closes in sheer exaggeration. In two 1900 productions by Brighton film-maker George Albert Smith, *The Dull Razor* and *A Quick Shave and Brush-Up*, the motivation for performer Tom Green's bizarre facial performance is an especially painful shave. 'As most men have had a similar experience', confirms a 1901 film catalogue, 'this subject is bound to create much mirth among an audience' (Warwick Catalogue 1901: 167).

The presence of music hall comedians such as Herbert Campbell and Tom Green suggests the source of this tradition of performance within the facials genre. At the turn of the century the stars of the halls were regularly celebrated for their mastery of facial pantomime – a mode of performance that also appeared in the fairground at this time. Indeed, catalogue descriptions of most genres of early film frequently accentuated the realism or comic effect of facial expression. For example, the 1897/98 Warwick Catalogue advertised many of Robert Paul's films, like *A Lively Dispute* (1898) and *The Twins' Tea Party* (1898) – both variations on the 'fight scene' – in terms of the effectiveness of their facial performances. 'Their expressions are most amusing and realistic', stressed the description of the former, though a full range of bodily gesture was presupposed by the main business of these pictures (Warwick Catalogue 1897–98: 23). But in facials, moving picture technology also enabled an exaggeration of this performance tradition, bringing a new emphasis to the details of the face and exploiting the grotesque effect of its magnification on the screen. This was particularly true in facials such as *'Herbert Campbell as Little Bobbie'*, Cecil Hepworth's *Macaroni Competition* (1899), the Warwick Trading Company's *The Yokel's Dinner* (1900) or George Albert Smith's *The Hungry Countryman* (1899), in which the spectacle of prodigious and messy consumption was at the heart of the entertainment.[4]

By 1907, when Robert Paul released a rather belated series of 'studies of facial expression', little had changed stylistically or technically within the genre, and *Kinematograph and Lantern Weekly* reviews for these films have an equivocal edge. '"Pity the Poor Blind"', according to one pointed review, 'has the virtue of moderate length in addition to the humour which it gains from good acting' ('Latest Productions', *The Kinematograph and Lantern Weekly*, 29 August 1907: 253–4). Paul's *How a Burglar Feels* (1907), at only 98 feet, was an extremely short film for the time and depended simply on the changing expressions of a 'very clever actor' responding to his capture by the police (R. W. Paul catalogue supplement, May 1907). Over a ten-year period otherwise characterised by rapid and unpredictable developments in film form and style, the narrative and thematic structures of this genre remained remarkably stable, and were beginning to appear exhausted.

The profound influence of the music hall tradition as re-interpreted and re-presented by the facials genre is apparent in films throughout the silent period. Exaggerated facial expression remained especially important for a tradition of movie 'clowning' in the 1910s and 1920s, as mastered by performers such as Florence Turner and Ben Turpin. In Turner's 1914 British film *Daisy Doodad's Dial* (Turner Film Company, 1914), Daisy attempts to enter an 'ugly-face' competition, but her mugging lands her in trouble with her husband and the police. The film demonstrates an unusually direct link between narrative film-making and a period when facial grimaces rather than naturalistic acting styles predominated.[5] An early guide to screenwriting offers another testament to Turner's facial skills within narrative film-making, this time in Vitagraph's *Jealousy* (1911):

> In it, Miss Florence Turner was the only actor, telling the whole story clearly, coherently, and with strong dramatic force, and making every phase of the plot clear, the only outside assistance she received being the momentary appearance of two other hands than her own – a man's and a woman's – through the curtains covering the doorway. This, of course, was pure pantomime, and most artistically performed; the woman's every thought, so to say, was portrayed, and understood by the audience as if the play were accompanied by a printed synopsis of the story. (Esenswein & Leeds 1913: 170–1)

The facials genre, derived from a longstanding nineteenth-century perform-ance tradition, would ultimately be reflected in the celebration of individual movie stars, like Florence Turner, for whom the lengthy facial close-up was both an opportunity to 'touch' their audiences and the ultimate accolade of their star status on the silver screen. Other performance traditions, such as those associated with the nineteenth-century magic lantern lecture, would have an equally profound impact upon the structure and subjects of early film genres, as the following case study will demonstrate.

Case study 2: Buy your own Cherries (Robert Paul, 1904)

The magic lantern, an optical projection device with a history stretching back to the seventeenth century, has long been recognised by film historians as a predominant influence on early British cinema. In terms of the technology of projection, the style of exhibition, and the repertoire of subjects represented, magic lantern culture of the late nineteenth century is easily compared to early film culture (Rossell 1998: 152–3). The format of the lantern shows varied dramatically. 'Dissolving views' magic lantern exhibitions, for example, delivered an illusionist spectacle to audiences wherein a winter landscape would be gradually transformed into a summer scene, or day into night, with the help of a complex projecting lantern apparatus. But by the 1890s most lantern shows involved the projection of a series of photographic lantern slides onto a screen in a simple narrative sequence. At the turn of the nineteenth century, the largest industrial producer of lantern slides, the Bamforth Company of Holmfirth, Yorkshire, were producing their slides in a studio similar to those that would subsequently be constructed by moving picture companies. Their catalogues of this period advertise genres of slide sequences strongly reminiscent of the early film catalogues, including subsections such as 'humorous subjects', 'slides from nature' and 'illustrated songs'. In fact, in partnership with Riley Brothers of Bradford, a company who had been involved with the technology of moving pictures since 1896, Bamforth were also responsible for a sequence of films produced in the 1898–1900 period. Some of these, including *Women's Rights*, which we have previously addressed in terms of the evidence it provides of a strand of social commentary in film-making, were derived directly from earlier Bamforth slide series.

Many lantern shows in the 1890s were intended to support illustrated songs – a relationship that would continue into the 1910s. But arguably most significant, in terms of the later development of early film, were the 'life model' slide sequences, in which the story told by photographic slides was supported by an accompanying lecture, usually serving moral, religious and temperance themes. Indeed, religious societies such as the Band of Hope Union, a powerful temperance group for children, made regular use of the magic lantern as a tool of moral instruction. In this context, it is not surprising that such groups were equally eager to adopt the cinematograph into their presentations, nor that British film-makers sought to develop and exploit this pre-established marketplace for their films.

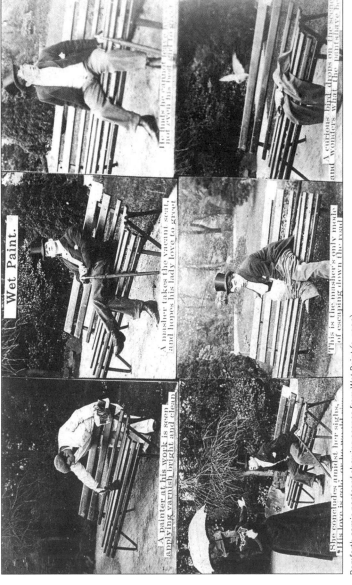

Bamforth comic postcard showing scenes from Wet Paint (c. 1900).

Robert Paul's *Buy your own Cherries* (1904) is a typical example of British temperance film-making from the beginning of the century. In just over four minutes this multi-shot film tells a remarkably complex story in which a working man learns that by shunning the public house he can provide properly for his wife and can even buy expensive treats, such as cherries, for the children. He is transformed from an abusive drunkard, whose own impoverished children are terrified of him, to a well-heeled gentleman, whose wife greets him home with a warm embrace, a well-stocked table and the promise of every home comfort. The film repeats a popular *fin-de-siècle* morality tale in which the perils of drink must be overcome in order to preserve health, family life, society at large and, therefore, in order to achieve a happy ending for audiences.

The story was almost certainly familiar to most of its audiences in this period. It was derived from an extremely well-known narrative that had already appeared in several magic lantern entertainments under the same title. Some of these included songs, or appended new details to the familiar storyline. Among the most sophisticated was a 36-slide set of *Buy your own Cherries*, which was accompanied by a lecture written by J. W. Kirton and published under the auspices of the Band of Hope Review Office. The lecture recounts the salvation of a carpenter called John Lewis, who successfully defeats his drinking habit – along with an especially vindictive landlady, in spite of her vow to 'lay traps to catch him before long' (Kirton n.d.: 8). Finding solace in temperance meetings, John provides for his children, and, free from 'the cursed drink', rises to a position of remarkable (and unlikely) eminence:

Step by step he rose, until he became a master of himself. Instead of working, he could pay other men to look after it and do it for him. He sent his son Tommy to a first-rate school; and in due time he was apprenticed to a doctor, and became a physician. The rest of the children were well educated. He built a nice row of houses, from which he received sufficient to keep him without work; and in a handsome 'villa', which he also built, he might often be seen reclining in an easy chair, viewing a cherry tree, which he planted with his own hands, and on which he had been able to '*grow his own cherries.*' He and his wife added to their temperance that Godliness which is profitable unto all things.

WORKING MEN! It is not how much money a week you earn, but *what you do with it* when you get it! How many a home comfort, such as carpets, sofas, chairs, and books, are lost by spending the money the wrong way. Learn from this tale of real life that the *outside* of a public-house is the *best* side, and if you wish to have a 'Home, sweet home',
'BUY YOUR OWN CHERRIES!' (Kirton n.d.: 16)

While the lecturer sermonised this moral, the last three slides appeared on the screen, as if confirming the truth of the story. It is also likely that a similar lecture might have accompanied the screening of Paul's film, perhaps, once again, within the context of temperance meetings. Thus, the highly developed storyline, the likely exhibition style, the content, theme and moral of the film are all closely related to the earlier magic lantern entertainment. We may regard the film as a close adaptation of earlier versions of *Buy your own Cherries* and can begin to uncover the evolution of the early genre of temperance film-making within this development. In this genre, complex stories of sin and redemption are told, and powerful moral messages are inevitably allied to bourgeois happy endings. Furthermore, the middle-class living and prosperity that were the rewards of sobriety in this tale suggest the reward structure at work in many classical narratives. The stories told by the nineteenth-century novel may have been more complex and usually revolved around different issues, but the clichéd denouement where the bad are punished and the good rewarded is also at work in *Buy your own Cherries*.

Stories and storytelling traditions

The performance of the lecturer in early cinema was only the most obvious mechanism for delivering a simple storyline to audiences. As the case of

Buy your own Cherries has clearly demonstrated, the storytelling potential of the projected image itself had already undergone several decades of development before the appearance of the first Lumière pictures in 1895. Even illusionist 'dissolving view' lantern entertainments already implied a basic narrative progression as one scene dissolved into another.

For film theorist and historian André Gaudreault, following a series of literary theorists of narrative, the characteristics of transformation and succession within such entertainments are already sufficient conditions for the existence of a basic form of visual story that would reappear in the first productions of the cinematograph (Gaudreault 1990a: 68–75).[6] According to this argument, a story can be simply defined as any scenario with a before and an after: one situation or state of affairs is subjected to change, and hence converted into a second situation or state of affairs. In this sense, even *'Herbert Campbell as Little Bobbie'* may be regarded as a narrative film: we are shown a simple story in which the hungry Campbell empties his plate and thus sates his considerable appetite.

In order to distinguish between these basic stories and the much more sophisticated feature film stories that developed within the first twenty years of cinema, we must be both more precise in our analysis of early film narratives and more inclusive in our historical review of earlier storytelling traditions. As theorists such as Gaudreault have often shown, the structures of story films are derived from universally understood principles of storytelling with a venerable heritage. But which storytelling traditions bore most influence upon early cinema? And how can we best understand their transformation onto the screen and their subsequent rapid development in the years before 1914?

Gaudreault suggests that even the first film-makers were necessarily aware of the potential narrative attractions of their productions. Traditions of storytelling derived from magic lantern lectures were particularly influential, as we have already seen. However, nineteenth-century theatrical and novelistic traditions were perhaps far more pervasive, though less visible, influences on the development of cinematic storytelling. The great volume of film adaptations derived from literary works in this period attests to the significance of this heritage. *Oliver Twist*, for example, was adapted at least nine times to the screen in the years between 1898 and 1913, and Shakespeare's *Hamlet* no less than ten times (Gifford 1991). Popular and well-known stories were thus regularly re-circulated in ever more sophisticated forms for the patrons of the moving pictures.

However, in the intermedial environment of early cinema culture before 1914, the stories told by the projected image, the performers on-screen and the film lecturer were all substantially influenced by the form as well as the content of these earlier texts and traditions. In this light, the primary significance of the regular film productions of *Oliver Twist* is that this novel typifies the tradition of nineteenth-century novelistic narrative, in which the narrator seems to 'disappear' and the reader, like the spectator in the movie theatre, becomes more and more immersed in the story. Borrowing from a series of literary studies of narrative in the novel and in theatre, Gaudreault has developed such insights into a formalist account of narrative development in early film. According to this account, early film combined theatrical traditions of performance that predominated in the first ten years of cinema with literary traditions of narration associated with the gradual sophistication of story films (Gaudreault 1990b: 276). Put simply, in the period 1895–1914, Gaudreault traces a development from a cinema in which film audiences, like audiences in the theatre, were simply *shown* the action on-screen, to one in which, like the readers of novels, they were *told* about significant actions within the storyline. In order to explore this important, but difficult, distinction between showing and telling in early film, we now offer two case studies that exemplify these modes of storytelling.

Case study: He and She (British Mutoscope and Biograph Company, 1899)

In this simple, one-shot film, a frantic argument is conducted between an elderly husband and his young wife. The late return of 'He' to the family home sparks a hysterical reaction from 'She', and as accusations and counter-accusations fly, the two pace vigorously back and forth across the scene. At one moment, He angrily smashes a plate and physically stands tall in the centre of the frame; meanwhile, She doubles up in tears at the left edge of the frame. Violently taking her revenge, She all but forces him out of the frame to the right, and secures the position of mastery in centre frame. Thus, within a swiftly fluctuating succession of reciprocal relationships on-screen that make full use of the limited *mise-en-scène*, He and She enact a simple storyline. Eventually, mollified by the gift He has brought her, She collapses gratefully back into his arms, and the film ends with an unlikely reconciliation. At this point, He turns significantly to the camera, sharing a gesture of masculine victory – and a joke on his wife – with the audience.

He and She presents a single, relatively lengthy shot, without camera movement, editing or inter-titling, but audiences are nonetheless given a great deal of story information concerning the marital tiff. The camera records the actions of the two characters as if they were performing on-stage to a live audience. In Gaudreault's terms, audiences of the film are *shown* all of the important information and, with no explicit attempt being made to narrate this information to them, are brought to a coherent, if rather stereotyped, understanding of the motivations of its characters. For modern audiences, the interpretation of *He and She* is therefore almost entirely dependent on the performances of its two actors. Indeed, within the static frame of this film, there is very little else to interpret. Their performances, as Gaudreault expresses it, enable them to 'tell the story by living it, right there in front of the audience. The need for intervention by a narrator does not arise' (1990a: 276).

Played by famous music hall artistes Frank M. Wood and Miss Roma, and adapted from their popular comic sketch of *He and She*, first performed in 1894, the scene called upon a specific style of acting strongly associated with the variety theatres in this period (Brown & Anthony 1999: 221, 258). This 'histrionic' style, characterised by Roberta Pearson, depended upon grand, exaggerated bodily gestures from performers and was intended to communicate a limited range of emotional states and attitudes to audiences (Pearson 1992: 38–43). Such audiences already fully understood these gestural conventions and were able to interpret them consistently. Thus the wife's hysterical response to her husband, telegraphed by her flailing arms and frantic pacing back and forth across the screen, might be read as evidence of a definitively feminine form of anger and distress. Similarly, enduring the worst of the attack from his wife, He runs both hands through his hair in a formal gesture of irritation; his return to favour is marked by the open embrace that was first denied him.

Cinematic *showing* in *He and She* thus depended upon its audience's familiarity with gestural performance conventions, and upon their recognition of key cultural stereotypes such as the 'shrewish wife' and the 'henpecked husband'. Other films at this time depended on different stereotypes: the 'mischievous child' drives the narrative of films like George Albert Smith's *The House that Jack Built* (1900); in Bamforth's *Weary Willie* (1898), the 'devious tramp' music hall persona appears, frightening off the well-heeled occupants of a park bench so that he can take a nap on it.[7] Traditional stereotypes and intertextual expectations therefore furnished audiences with a range of conventions concerning the characters and narratives of films such as *He and She*. Audiences already knew a great deal about the warring husband and wife of this film – to the extent that it did not matter if these universally recognised characters remained anonymous, appropriately identified only by their genders.

However, while much of the action in the film is delivered in a histrionic mode, there is also, occasionally, the promise of a more individualising representation of character. As She reads the letter, before the argument begins, and again, after the two are reconciled, her minute play of gesture opens into possibilities for naturalistic forms of characterisation – a style of performance usually associated with the legitimate theatre and with the moving picture in its post-1908 developments. This potential for character psychology is realised during appealing moments of ambiguity where characters escape histrionic acting practices. 'Gesture is the direct agent of the heart', wrote the influential nineteenth-century theorist and teacher of theatrical acting, François Delsarte, and there is a scant suggestion of this intimate expressiveness at points in *He and She*.[8] The film points us toward a different kind of cinematic *showing*, in which actors no longer need to alert us to moments of narrative significance, but become psychologically complex components within a greater storytelling system.

Case study: Rescued by Rover (Hepworth Manufacturing Co., 1905)

The system of cinematic *telling* that, according to Gaudreault, would come to dominate the cinema depended upon the development of editing conventions in the years after 1898. Although the single-shot film dominated international film production until around 1906, the ability for the camera to move between different scenes at different locations, or to fragment the space within a scene using a variety of long shots, medium shots, and close-ups, also opened up new possibilities for early cinema's representation of space and time (Salt 1992: 31–61). No longer constrained to show only the events passing before the lens of the camera during a single take, film-makers began to experiment with combining two or more shots within each film, and soon learned that they could *tell* complex stories by simply passing from one image to the next. Spectators now had to determine the relationship between each shot, and in doing so began to intuit a narrative 'presence' – a narrator – that seemed to be responsible for arranging these shots into a coherent story. Of course, this principle was familiar from magic lantern sequences like *'Buy Your Own Cherries'*, and often the film's narrator would be embodied during exhibition by a lantern-style lecturer, who could explain directly the logic of these shot sequences to early audiences unfamiliar with the convention. Elsewhere, the projection of occasional magic lantern 'announcement' slides between films was sometimes used to explain the forthcoming action to audiences. In the following years the image track itself began to take primary responsibility for this storytelling practice, both by the introduction of inter-titling in the years after 1904 and, most significantly, by the conventionalisation of film editing principles into a recognisable vocabulary of shots and shot transitions within fictional storytelling film genres.

In fact, the basic technical principle of cutting and joining film had been understood from as early as 1895. The early trick films of Georges Méliès also often made use of cutting 'in the camera', in which the camera was simply stopped in the middle of an action, and then started again once the scene had been changed in some way. In this way, objects could be 'magically' made to appear or disappear with no obvious sleight of hand. However, the chief concern of these illusionist editing principles was to make the manipulation of the image track invisible to audiences, who were left wondering how the trick could have been realised. Our modern understanding of editing as a kind of film grammar allowing for subtle manipulations of space and time developed only slowly in the years that followed. As Barry Salt has shown, the use of shot sequences intended to represent two adjacent spaces probably began with Robert Paul's celebrated *Come Along, Do!* (1898), in which an elderly couple are shown taking lunch outside a gallery and then are shown examining the exhibits within (Salt 1992: 36). The early genre of 'chase films', first developed by James Williamson's *Stop Thief!* (1901), in which the protagonists careered after one another across a series of shots, demonstrates that continuity of action between scenes was becoming an increasingly conventional part of the film-maker's vocabulary.

By 1900, George Albert Smith had developed a method of dissecting a single scene into a number of shots. *Grandma's Reading Glass* (1900) demonstrates a basic form of point-of-view sequence, in which the objects seen by a small boy through a magnifying glass are shown in sequence to the audience. The voyeuristic implications of such films were subsequently developed more fully in 'peeping tom' films like *Par le Trou de Serrure* (Pathé, 1901) in which the point of view of a young man looking through keyholes into a series of private rooms was presented to audiences.

To some extent, these practices of film editing may be seen as a response to early film exhibitors, who sometimes played films in narrative sequence, perhaps making the continuity of action apparent to audiences with a spoken lecture. As early as 1898, the Warwick Trading Company had advertised a sequence of four films, collectively entitled *The Big Fire*, which 'should be joined in the order mentioned, and when so projected reproduce one of the most exciting scenes ever presented', the relevant scene depicting the fire-brigade responding to an emergency (Warwick Catalogue 1897–98: 51). James Williamson's *Fire!* (1901) and Edwin S. Porter's celebrated *Life of an American Fireman* (Edison, 1903) were multi-shot films based upon the same subject and may be seen as a development by film-makers of this earlier exhibition stratagem.

Rescued by Rover (Hepworth Manufacturing Company, 1905) exploited many of the established conventions of film editing, combining them with earlier performance traditions with a clarity and style that would become increasingly characteristic of early film production. Produced by Lewis Fitzhamon for Cecil Hepworth's company, this multi-shot film, lasting just over six minutes, stars the Hepworth family in the thrilling story of a baby's kidnap and its rescue by the family dog, the eponymous Rover. Let us now subject the film to a detailed scene-by-scene analysis in order to see how its continuity of action and stylistic polish was accomplished:

Opening tableau of baby and dog
This shot exemplifies the well-established convention for early films to begin and/or end with an emblematic shot, in which the central theme or preoccupation of the film is simply, and often metaphorically, presented to audiences. In this brief tableau, Rover is seen 'standing guard' over a baby lying in the foreground, thus establishing the key relationship between the child and its protector that will drive the storyline forwards.

Scene 1: in the park
In this two-shot scene, a woman wearing a nursemaid's outfit pushes a pram, presumably containing the same child as seen in the opening tableau, through a park. In shot one, in the foreground, a beggar woman – another contemporary popular stereotype – approaches the nurse for money, which is haughtily refused, the nurse telegraphing her distaste with her nose turned upwards. As the nurse traverses the screen from left to right, the beggar remains centre-frame shaking her fists in fury. As in all shots in the movie, camera movement is minimal, and used only to accommodate the movement of figures within the frame.

In shot two, the nurse is again seen walking from left to right, thus suggesting continuous action from the previous shot. With her back turned to the pram, she is distracted from her charge by the romantic attentions of a young man. Meanwhile, the beggar approaches, this time from a hedge in the background, and steals the child.

Scene 2: at home
A woman sits at home conducting her domestic duties. The nurse enters, bewailing the fate of the lost child, thus establishing a narrative connection with the previous scene in the park and the identity of the new character – evidently the mother of the child. Meanwhile, Rover, who has been listening attentively, runs out of the same door into a new narrative space.

Scene 3: the chase
Having left the house, Rover enters the street, thus confirming spatial continuity between the interior set and the well-to-do neighbourhood. In a series of four shots, Rover runs through the streets and swims across a canal, before arriving at a row of working class back-to-back houses. In each shot, he runs towards the camera, thus confirming his progress through contiguous spaces towards his destination. In the poor neighbourhood he stops, trying each of the doors before finally entering one at the end of the row.

Scene 4: interior of beggar's room
The beggar woman appears, carrying the baby, in an unfurnished and ramshackle room, beautifully lit so that shadows are cast ominously across it. Settling initially at the far right of the frame, she steals most of the clothes from the child, placing them to the left of the frame. She now moves centre-frame to take a nap, thus restoring balance to the composition. Now Rover enters from the right, and we realise that in the previous shot he had discovered the correct house. Rover is chased from the room.

Scene 5: the return
In a reversal of scene 3, four shots of the same locations are now shown with Rover running and swimming away from the camera. We deduct that he means to return home.

Scene 6: back at home
Back in the interior of the family home, a man, hand on forehead, telegraphs his anxieties to audiences. Clearly this is the child's father.

105

Rover enters from the streets and, after repeated attempts, succeeds in convincing Father to follow him (pausing to put on his top hat and coat!).

Scene 7: to the rescue

The series of shots from scene 3 is repeated, now with Rover and Father running towards the camera. Arriving at the canal, Father takes a boat across. The camera pans slightly in order to keep these actions within the frame, and thus provide all relevant information concerning the rescue to audiences. Arriving at the beggar's house, Father turns with a gesture of astonishment to the camera, and pointing through the doorway, follows Rover inside. This gesture brings the performance tradition of direct address to the storyline, which otherwise constitutes a perfectly self-enclosed narrative.

Scene 8: the beggar's room again

Rover and the Father disturb the beggar in her room. Recovering his child, Father leaves the beggar to console herself with the clothing she has taken.

Scene 9: together again

Father, child, and Rover return to the family home. The journey between the two houses is not shown this time: without the tension of the rescue to interest audiences it is removed altogether, bringing the storyline to its satisfyingly abrupt denouement. In shot one of this two-shot scene, Mother's hysteria changes remarkably quickly to domestic contentment, as the family settle into a balanced family portrait. Shot two reframes the action in close-up, and is an example of a 'cut-in', here leaving audiences with a final tableau of the reunited family, Rover included.

As this scene-by-scene description makes clear, *Rescued by Rover* depended upon a wide range of conventions of continuity editing between scenes, but also exploited earlier histrionic conventions of acting in order to convey story information efficiently to its spectators. All of the central characters make use of grand gestures in order to express their emotions and motivations to audiences. Furthermore, the interactions between characters, such as the uncharitable response of the nursemaid to the beggar in scene 2, are so clearly telegraphed that further description is unnecessary.

A great deal of care is taken to balance the frame compositionally, giving the viewer few unnecessary distractions from the complicated line of action depicted. Furthermore, deep space is used efficiently throughout the film. In scene 2, the beggar approaches the nurse from the foreground and then from the background, increasing our sense that this predatory woman is in control of the space and may creep up unseen if she wishes. In scenes 3, 5 and 7, deep space is used to show the rapid progress of Rover between the two houses and also to demonstrate the direction in which he is travelling as he approaches or retreats from the camera. The editing between the shots in these scenes is strongly reminiscent of the 'chase films' genre, demonstrating continuity of action between adjacent spaces. Similarly, the progress of various characters between interior and exterior spaces is now marked by the convention of having them enter or exit a doorway, followed by a cut to the same character in a new space. Furthermore, the film trusts its audiences to competently recognise characters and spaces they have seen in previous scenes, repeatedly showing them the two neighbourhoods, the two houses and the film's distinctively dressed characters, and allowing them to discern the complex relationships between them.

Finally, the intricately constructed continuity of action, which successfully tells this adventure story from beginning to end, is successfully 'framed' and closed by the tableau shots that begin and end the picture, offering us a conventional and humorous happy ending as the family are reunited. There is also a strong suggestion within these shots of a narrative presence behind the film. For example, in the final scene, the cut-in to a close-up family portrait offers us no further story information; however, there is a suggestion that this shot is strongly motivated by an intention to emphasise the family settling back into domestic security. As in *Buy your own Cherries* and in fiction film generally in this period, we are left with the impression that an organised and distinctly moral consciousness guides the action of this picture, telling us what the narrative relationship between shots might be and efficiently guiding our reactions through its suspenseful progress from beginning to end.

This kind of relationship with spectators, which asked that they passively followed the *telling* of a story, would gradually become dominant in the years before 1910. British film-makers were relatively early in their development of the new idiom of film, perhaps because of the powerful influence of magic lantern storytelling tradition. However, by 1907, developments in the US and especially in France were beginning to make the British film industry look parochial and primitive by comparison. As Richard Abel has exhaustively shown, Pathé's domestic melodramas in the 1905–7 period were instrumental in the popularisation of a more fluid form of film grammar in which camera movement and changes in framing began to serve rhetorical representational strategies. Within this 'loose system of representation and narration' techniques such as cut-ins and reverse-angle cutting were increasingly used to accentuate key dramatic motifs and actions (Abel 1994: 136). From 1907, these editing techniques began to serve similar discursive purposes in other genres in the Pathé catalogue. They would soon be adopted by other French and US film-makers. The process of cinematic *telling* at work in such films now began to present spectators with a standardised articulation of space and time, one that did not wholly rely on audiences' active application of local knowledge. As this passive practice of spectatorship became more dominant, so the patterns of film production, exhibition and spectatorship associated with the multi-shot film underwent fundamental changes.

Narrative, genre and spectatorship: the picture theatres and the development of feature film

The development of film as a self-enclosed, and increasingly fictional, medium had several powerful and related effects upon the development of the industry. Firstly, it engineered a different viewing position for audiences, whose often noisy and collaborative responses to the earliest exhibitions of film were gradually supplanted by the silent activity of discerning the logic and sequence of the action on-screen. Secondly, this close attention paid to the activities on-screen tended to preclude attention to live performances. If the moving picture had often been merely illustrative of the educational discourse of a lecturer, by 1908, the lecturer had mostly become a mere 'describer' of the action onscreen. Responsibility for the success of the films had effectively moved backwards through the industrial process from the exhibitors to the film-makers. Thirdly, as a result of this transition, the films themselves began to develop elements of style or 'personality' that previously had been conveyed directly to audiences by the showmen, and these were associated especially with fictional genres of narrative film-making. One aspect of this was the rapid development of a star system in film, especially in the US, from about 1908 (deCordova 1990); another was an increasingly subtle generic differentiation between the different kinds of stories told by films; a third was the development of feature films, sometimes of epic length, whose style was subtly but consistently personalised.

The early film student may trace these developments across a series of parallel histories of film production, exhibition, and reception. However, as Nicholas Hiley (1998) has demonstrated, the development of picture palaces in the UK in the 1910s and of new and consistent viewing strategies from audiences were closely linked to the emergence of feature film production. An important 1909 article from *The World's Fair* also describes the close connection between the emergence of the 'miniature theatres' in London and the longer 'miniature dramas' that were preoccupying film producers (*The World's Fair*, 9 January 1909: 7). Seeking now to increase the demand for such dramas, the business plans of film producers revolved around the development of narrative scenarios within their films. A series of guidebooks to screenwriting proliferated from this time, such as Eustace Hale Ball's American publication, *The Art of the Photoplay* (1913), seeking to answer the growing demand for screenplays. An early British example of advice to the aspiring screenwriter suggests the increasingly expert management of a film's narrative resources:

The story of a picture, humorous or dramatic, must be very clear and easily followed. A simple line of progressive action, through a series of scenes must be maintained until the climax is reached, each scene having a definite connection with the story.

Do not introduce too many important characters; and – this most important – try to arrange your scenes [sic] 'real exteriors' – as gardens, streets, lanes, sea-beach, &c. When it is necessary to introduce an 'interior', have it as simple as possible. Film manufacturers keep a stock company of experienced actors and actresses, but it must be remembered these people, clever as they may be, are limited entirely to 'dumb show' and pure pantomime to tell their story.

Work your plot out in numbered scenes, each having a definite incident. The probability of acceptance is greater with light comedy stories, with just a touch of pathos, in a picturesque setting. (Anon. 1911b: 11)

Thus, as early as 1911, the 'recipe' for a successful plot was already in place. The ideal scenario described a succession of scenes, each with its own centre of narrative interest, in which audiences easily understood the performances of actors within each shot and were also able to follow the narrative connection between shots. The basic principles of narrative continuity we have discovered at work in *Rescued by Rover* were thus fully systematised and now yielded further diversifications in film form, spectatorship and manufacture.

It was not simply the case that the desire of audiences for simple and dramatic storylines was alone responsible for the change toward fictional output. By 1909, the production of story film genres also offered distinct advantages for the increasingly industrial mechanisms of film manufacture. Indeed, according to one of a new breed of picture theatre trade journals, the 'regular business' of the film-maker began with 'the finding of plots and stories' that were likely to be popular but could be easily and cheaply staged (Anon. 1909c: 21). The stories then passed through distinct stages of pre-production, shooting, post-production, and distribution to an increasingly US-centred marketplace. An efficient and rational division of labour by process supplanted the artisanal practices of film-makers like James Williamson or George Albert Smith. A growing number of professionals filled ever more specialised roles in the production and were able to turn out complex pictures far more quickly than had been possible for earlier generations of film-makers.

Thus, the growth and consolidation of storytelling practices in early film responded not only to the demands of spectators, for whom simple pictorial stories, such as those in magic lantern shows, had long been an attraction of entertainment institutions, but also to the requirements of industrial rationalisation. In particular, the necessity for film-makers to obtain intellectual property rights on their pictures and prevent copying by competitors had a powerful influence on the types of films they chose to produce. It was important that each film contained unique characteristics that differentiated it from the rest of contemporary film production. These considerations especially favoured the continuing dominance of fictional story films. The content and form of these films could be easily defended because it was possible to isolate within them a form of creative storytelling akin to the creative work of literary authors or of theatrical producers.[9] Alongside a growing dependence on movie stars and celebrities, the film studios therefore sought especially to specialise the narratives of their films, and, like generations of literary authors before them, were quite prepared to defend their ownership of stories in the courts. From 1908, the Berlin Conference on international copyright conventions clarified for the first time in Europe that 'Cinematographic productions shall be protected as literary or artistic works if, by the arrangement of the acting form or the combination of incidents represented, the author has given the work a personal and original character' (Ricketson 1986: 550–1).

Thus, storytellers were not only a long-familiar attraction for spectators, they also represented a form of agency that was recognised, owned and defended in the courts. The development of identifiable film styles would ultimately be reflected in the high-culture identification and commodification of directors as the 'authors' of film. By 1914, however, it had already initiated developments in the variety and content of film genres that were available to the public. While comic subjects, actualities, newsreels and travelogues now represented only a small proportion of movie production, more fictional narrative genres began to develop. Genres of romance, adventure, melodrama and comedy, initially derived from a range of earlier traditions, now reappeared on-screen in increasingly sophisticated narrative scenarios. The film serial, drawing out a melodramatic narrative across many episodes, would typically leave its heroine stranded in the cliff-hanger ending of each. Its audiences, hooked on the sequential storyline, would have to wait to discover how she would be rescued on each occasion. In *The Perils of Pauline* (Louis J. Gasnier and Donald MacKenzie, 1914), Pauline's adventures led to her rescue from the deep sea, hot-air balloons, horse and motorcar races, and all manner of dangerous criminal environments, only to leave her at the mercy of some new peril next time around.

As the stylistic competence of the image track grew in stature and maturity, other, high-cultural aspirations of film led to the evolution of the confessedly literary form of the 'photo-play'. In France, from 1908, the Film D'Art company initiated a series of productions of historical and literary subjects. Borrowing strongly from Pathé's earlier development of editing conventions within their domestic melodramas, these productions became equally influential in their own right, introducing 'a newer system of representation', as Abel describes it, 'negotiating a balanced orchestration of *mise-en-scène*, framing, editing patterns, and even sound accompaniment' (Abel 1994: 277). These films self-consciously presented high-cultural discourses associated with literary and historical intertexts, telling complex stories and using diversifying conventions of film grammar. Soon afterwards, the US-based Vitagraph company also began to specialise in these 'quality' productions, bringing numerous classic novels and plays to the screen (Pearson & Uricchio 1993). Borrowing authority from the 'great figures' of literature also enabled the Picture Palaces to appeal to new – and richer – audiences. 'Theatre owners', wrote one British commentator, 'will do well to cultivate the tastes of their audiences by gradually increasing the number of high class film subjects, thus cutting down the demand for some of the rubbish sold as comics' (Anon. 1911c: 51). In the US, where film production was already at a stage of considerable institutional advancement, this 'gentrification' of narrative film was played out on an industrial scale:

> The road shows of theatrical successes have received decreasing interest with each succeeding month. Lamentable as this may seem it has its benefits for the American play-goer. Through the medium of the cinematograph one good production, presented by the best obtainable artists, and under the most perfect conditions attainable is seen by sixteen millions in a year, as against one hundred thousand who would see a successful play in the same time. (Ball 1913: 117)

An assumption is made here that the spectator of the film is still, in all appropriate senses, a 'play-goer' and that the film was therefore capable of representing the same complex narrative structures that had appeared in the theatre. This carries with it the economic significance of an exponential increase in spectatorship for the 'play' under conditions of mechanical reproduction enabled by the cinematograph. Raking in money from an increasingly international audience enabled film producers to invest much more heavily in their films than had ever been possible in the theatre, and many were staged on a spectacular scale. When, in 1911, Carl Laemmle's IMP Film Co. adapted famous nineteenth-century playwright Dion Boucicault's melodrama, *The Long Strike*, to the screen, much of the melodramatic storyline, involving a pair of star-crossed lovers and an industrial dispute, remained intact. However, in addition to the succession of obviously 'stagey' scenes played out between the melodramatic villain, the hero and the heroine, the film also included an entirely new scene, in which one character dives fifty feet into the water from the deck of an immense passenger liner. This stunt, actually enacted by Herbert Brennon, the film's director, was central to advertising for the film, and brought an entirely new attraction to an otherwise lacklustre storyline. As the melodrama developed from the stage into more sophisticated and lengthy productions on-screen, genre conventions gradually began to alter, bringing new, costly and spectacular attractions, as well as new types of storyline, to its audience.

The audience too was changing. In 1912, as Hiley has noted, most film exhibitors in the UK ran a continuous show for audiences, most of whom would enter from the street in order to sit down and relax (Hiley 1998: 98). The film would run continuously through the projector so that patrons could sit and watch the entire programme, if they so chose, perhaps leaving when they recognised the film that they first saw upon entering. By 1914, many exhibitors in the picture theatres would run discrete but lengthy programmes, perhaps only twice a day, selling tickets to audiences who would then watch a series of films from beginning to end. Many of these films were still only five or ten minutes in length; however, at the top of the bill were films of thirty minutes and more, for which a new generation of filmgoers had an increasing appetite.

This taste for longer narrative films, sometimes containing several distinct sub-plots and requiring their audiences to demonstrate a great deal of interpretational expertise, was ultimately satisfied by the rise of the 'feature film': the film that was literally the top billed feature on the programme. In 1912–13, the one- and even two-hour epic began to appear in the US and continental Europe and was followed by British producers shortly afterwards with a series of major literary adaptations and historical dramas such as *Oliver Twist* (1912), *East Lynne* (1913), *Ivanhoe* (1913), *The Battle of Waterloo* (1913) and *Little Lord Fauntleroy* (1914).

The development of the feature film has been most often associated with American film-maker, D. W. Griffith, a figure often credited as the pioneer of classical narrative strategies in film. Revisionist film historians, who have traced significant developments in film form to earlier film-makers, have justifiably challenged some aspects of Griffith's formidable reputation. More recently, Tom Gunning has demonstrated that 'landmark' films such as *Birth of a Nation* (1915), for which Griffith is best remembered, were the product of several years of experimentation in narrative form in which he had also taken a leading part (Gunning 1994). Incontrovertibly, however, *Birth of a Nation*, among several movies in this period, demonstrates the innovative and polished execution of influential techniques of story construction and cinematography.

Case study: Birth of a Nation (D. W. Griffith, 1915)

In the course of almost three hours, *Birth of a Nation* tells the complex story of two families, the Stonemans and the Camerons, who are divided by the American Civil War. Their interests, however, are ultimately reunited in their wish, embodied by the masked figures of Ku Klux Klansmen, to re-instate racial segregation after the abolition of slavery and thus return the American South to its 'natural order'. The explicitly racist message of the movie, which manipulated historical events in order to represent the Klan as American heroes, led immediately to its condemnation as propaganda by such organisations as the National Association for the Advancement of Colored People – a charge justifiably levelled throughout its exhibition history.

In spite of its controversial political message, which still makes *Birth* uncomfortable viewing for modern audiences, the film remains a powerful document. Among the many technical effects advanced by Griffith, his cameraman, Billy Bitzer, and others associated with the production, were scenes shot at night using magnesium flares for lighting, the abundant use of panoramic long-shots juxtaposed with intimate facial close-ups, and the application of extensive 'parallel editing', in which two simultaneous actions taking place in different spaces were cross-cut in order to create tension. *Birth* advanced a firm understanding of the storytelling potential of a wide variety of shot types, shot transitions and camera movements, allowing audiences to make sense of the spaces represented within these shots without any unintentional disorientation or discontinuity. The movie followed an easily discernible narrative trajectory in which audiences could trace the progress of key characters through the space and time of a key moment in US history. Thus, the principles of continuity editing, whose origins we can trace back to films like *Rescued by Rover*, *Buy your own Cherries* and, indeed, to two-shot movies before the turn of the century, are fully developed by *Birth of a Nation*. As historians of cinema, we can certainly regard this film as a 'landmark' in terms of its exploitation, innovation, and consolidation of feature film conventions.

These same conventions also mark the emergence of a powerful narrator 'within' or 'behind' the film whose unpalatable message concerning race is convincingly elaborated to audiences. Interweaving the intimate histories of two fictional white families with the epic historical representation of Civil War and race conflict, *Birth* triggers our empathy for these characters, but channels it to political ends. According to the story told by the film, the threat posed by untrustworthy, violent and sexually predatory African-American characters apparently justifies the violent response of the Klan members and the segregationist moral of the story. Indeed, this position is directly articulated in the film by the regular use of descriptive inter-titles, which declare at one point that the Ku Klux Klan was 'the organization that saved the South from the anarchy of black rule, but not without the shedding of more blood than at Gettysburg'.

The propagandist function of this film therefore depended upon its intricate extrapolation of family melodrama onto the epic stage of US history. Although, of course, not all audiences were convinced, the conspicuous financial success of the movie – fuelled by controversy as well as by an unprecedented two-dollar US ticket price – indicates the success of its intimate, biographical dramatisation of a still-divisive conflict. Its effect also depended upon the engineering of a delicately poised relationship between audience and narrative, reinforced by a specially composed score. The film's expert management of narrative resources led audiences through a pattern of conflict, climax and resolution that was reinforced by emotive music and which culminated in a sensational, rapid-paced, parallel-edited scene as the Klansmen ride to a last-minute rescue of the Cameron family. *Birth of a Nation* typifies what Thomas Elsaesser has described as a kind of 'audience-oriented aesthetic' in which audiences, restricted physically to their seats, ensconced in darkness, and no longer licensed to interact with live performers or other members of the audience, were compensated for these deprivations by three hours of programmed action voyeuristically experienced on-screen (Elsaesser 1981).

Of course, styles and conventions of storytelling have become more specialised and diverse, but this fundamental relationship between spectator and screen still governs traditions of mainstream cinema today.

However, as students of film history, we should also note that even this early example of classical film-making encouraged, rather than suppressed, critical debate and popular protest. While the film's management of its historical narrative seems dedicated to assuaging contemporary white, middle-class paranoia in the US concerning the growing political muscle of the African-American population, this was clearly not the only conclusion audiences drew. As in the first years of cinema, audiences persisted in interpreting films critically and, in conformity with key contextual and intertextual precedents, *Birth of a Nation* could be read variously as a celebration or a betrayal of the most cherished American democratic ideals. Although active discussion of the film's narrative and thematic content took place, by now, mostly outside the confines of the movie theatre, spectators persisted in their longstanding habit of critical interpretation. In this limited sense, at least, we may trace a direct line of continuity between the first audiences of the moving picture, bewildered, enchanted, and fascinated by the flickering images on the screen, and those of 1915, whose expertise and knowledge of narrative conventions in moving pictures had also initiated a parallel sophistication in their ability to interpret, reinterpret and evaluate what they saw.

Conclusion

The progression of genre and narrative conventions in the moving pictures drew substantially upon earlier traditions and media, which they subsequently adapted in the light of changing formal, institutional and commercial conditions. The often noisy and confrontational responses of the earliest audiences to film shows in variety theatres, fairgrounds and lecture theatres were certainly suppressed by the film's, and the picture theatre's, growing mastery of narrative techniques. But, in another significant sense, what followed in the years after 1914 was also a continuation of the earliest practices or film production, exhibition and reception. In spite of the rapid pace of the cinema's development and consolidation in the 1896–1914 period, it remained and, indeed, remains in the present day, committed to the effective satisfaction and management of its audiences' changing critical requirements. Co-ordinated principally with a commercial environment in which film-makers, exhibitors and spectators were all complicit, the early cinema inherited and bequeathed an impressive populist legacy. Arguably, traditions of popular entertainment, typified by the cinema throughout much of the twentieth century, have offered the most expansive environment for the negotiation and transformation of modern experience in this period. We believe that for the student of early cinema, the initial formulation of the medium represents a key transformative moment whose implications are still being played out, and which has much information and insight yet to offer us.

NOTES

Chapter 3

1 For an early example see Stephen Bottomore's (1984) account of the Dreyfus affair.
2 *The National Council of Public Morals Report 1917.*
3 'It is among our duties to see that good habits prevail among the clergy and to protect their morality. Having ascertained that members of the Regular and secular clergy attend Kinematograph spectacles, many of which offend religion and morality, we informed the Holy Father, who authorised us to remind the clergy that they may not frequent theatres, and that they are particularly ordered not to attend Kinematograph exhibitions of any kind. Any clergyman contravening this order will be liable to canonical punishment, including suspension from the celebration of mass and divine offices.' Catholic edict, reported in the *World's Fair*, 24 July 1909.
4 *The Thomas Edison Animated Pictures – China And Boer Wars – Letterhead* (1901): author's collection.

Chapter 4

1 In fact the cinematograph was used in a variety of combinations with the theatrical performance of actors onstage. The difficulty arose for

these productions when an effort was made to represent the screen as though it were a window onto reality. The screen was – obviously – just a screen. By contrast, in the successful 1905 production of *A Silent Accuser* at the Crown Theatre in Peckham, the plot directly involved the cinematograph itself, and this problem did not arise. This was a crime melodrama that depicted a murderer brought to justice because his crime had been filmed by a passing cinematographer. The cinematograph recorded and then revealed the heinous actions of the murderer for the benefit of both jury and audience.

2 'Prof. Stone', *The Showman* (21 June 1901), 395.

3 *Pathé Cinematograph Company catalogue* (May 1903), p. 39.

4 In fact, the introductions of new media have always been associated with this kind of distrust. This social response itself requires explanation, and the opportunity remains to conduct further research concerning such anxieties among assorted new media audiences. How can the first responses of audiences to film, television, or to the internet be compared?

5 'At England's Home of Mystery', *The Showman* (26 April 1901), 265–6.

6 The manuscript has been privately published, but even this curtailed version is extremely scarce. We refer to the complete manuscript, which can be found at the National Fairground Archive at the University of Sheffield, UK. In fact, the use of anecdote has been criticised by recent generations of film historians, who have argued that the details anecdotes 'reveal' are both unreliable and sometimes actively misleading. Although this is true, it does not altogether destroy the value of anecdotes derived from early film culture as a source of historical evidence. After all, even if the purpose of an anecdote is to deliberately mislead, then the motivations behind this deception may well prove to be of considerable interest. We must interpret such material carefully, but to ignore it altogether is to unjustifiably neglect a unique source of information.

7 For example consider George Pearson's relatively well-known recollections of the penny gaff cinematograph show, which especially emphasise the role of the showman:

'It was outside a derelict greengrocer's shop. The hawk-eyed gentleman on a fruit crate was bewildering a sceptical crowd. In that shuttered shop there was a miracle to be seen for a penny, but only twenty-four could enter at a time; there wasn't room for more. His peroration was magnificent; 'You've seen pictures of people in books, all frozen stiff. You've never seen people come alive in pictures, moving about natural like you and me. Well, go inside and see for yourself living pictures for a penny. Then tell me if I'm a liar.' George Pearson (1938) 'Lambeth Walk to Leicester Square', *Sight and Sound*, 7, 28, 150.

Chapter 5

1 For more information on this device, see Barry Anthony (1996) *The Kinora: Motion Pictures for the Home 1896–1914*. London: The Projection Box.

2 Arthur Sturgess and Arthur Collins (1899) *Theatre Royal, Drury Lane Grand Christmas Pantomime: Jack and the Beanstalk*. London: Nassau Press. See also the lengthy review in *The Era* (30 December 1899), 10. The pantomime is also of interest to film historians interested in popular reactions to the Boer War. In its final scene, the British army pour out of the pockets of the Giant Blunder-Boer – a withering reference to Krueger's well-known 1899 boast that he could fit the entire British army into one of his pockets.

3 For a more extensive account of this tradition see Tom Gunning (1997) 'In Your Face: Physiognomy, Photography, and the Gnostic Mission of Early Film', *MODERNISM/modernity* 4, 1–29; and Joe Kember (2001) 'Face-to-face: The Facial Expressions Genre in Early British Film', in Alan Burton and Laraine Porter (eds) *The Showman, the Spectacle, and the Two-Minute Silence: Performing British Cinema Before 1930*. Trowbridge: Flicks Books.

4 In fact *The Yokel's Dinner* and *The Hungry Countryman* added the attraction of the 'reversing subject' to this generic formula, delighting in the grotesque spectacle of performers retrieving food from their open mouths and laying it back on the plate.

5   For more information on Florence Turner, see Ann-Marie Cook (2000) 'The Adventures of the "Vitagraph Girl" in England', in Alan Burton and Laraine Porter (eds) *Pimples, Pranks, and Pratfalls: British Film Comedy Before 1930*. Trowbridge: Flicks Books, 34–5.

6   Gaudreault's most extensive discussions of this issue are conducted in his untranslated book-length study of early film narrative, *Du Littéraire au Filmique: Système du Récit* (Paris: Méridiens Klincksieck, 1988), which is available in several UK academic libraries. In this work, Gaudreault describes the minimal conditions for the existence of narrative ('*séquence narrative minimale*'), and then describes the increasing formal sophistication of early film narratives in the first years of cinema.

7   For further work on the implications of the idioms of music hall performance in early film, see Chanan 1996: 221–5.

8   François Delsarte (1887) 'Delsarte's Own Words' (taken from notes), in *Delsarte System of Oratory: Including the Complete Work of M. L'Abbe Delamosne and Mme. Angelique Arnaud (Pupils of Delsarte) with the Literary Remains of François Delsarte*. New York: Edgar S. Werner, 466. Delsarte's premier exponent in the UK was Gustave Garcia: see especially, Gustave Garcia (1882) *The Actor's Art: A Practical Treatise on Stage Declamation, Public Speaking and Deportment*. London: T. Pettitt, 113–66.

9   In the UK, an important case was brought by music hall performer Fred Karno against Pathé Frères, on the grounds that their film *At the Music Hall* (1906) infringed Karno's copyright on his sketch 'The Mumming Birds or Twice Nightly' under the 1833 Dramatic Copyright Act. Similarly, in the US, Lew Wallace sued the Kalem Company for their 16-scene film version of his *Ben Hur* (1907) under dramatic copyright legislation and, for the first time in such a challenge on the movies, succeeded.

SOURCES AND RESOURCES

It is of course impossible to list all potential sources of information for the history of early cinema, but we wish to identify some of the key and most accessible sources available to students.

The British Film Institute
This holds one of the largest collections of books and journals related to film in the world. Students should note that the use of the library is not free, and that it is advisable to book a seat in advance, especially if they are coming to London from a distance. The library catalogue is available on-line at: http://www.bfi.org.uk/nationallibrary/index.html. BFI Collections and Archive are also a crucial source of material and can be accessed online. They include a variety of searchable catalogues and information on the availability of prints and videos: http://www.bfi.org.uk/collections/index.html.

The British Library
This holds copies of every title published in the UK and is a vital source for finding rare publications. You can search the library catalogue at: http://www.bl.uk.

The Guildhall Library, London
Essential for the business historian since it holds the records of the London Stock Exchange, and, *inter alia*, a comprehensive collection of financial journals and newspapers including those generated in the 1895–1914 period. A primary source for the location of company prospectuses. Available on-line at: http://www.history.ac.uk/gh.

The Newspaper Library, Colindale, London
Much more than simply a newspaper library, this library holds many rare and unique late nineteenth-/early twentieth-century publications related to popular entertainment. Two essential hand lists are available on-line.

The British Library Newspaper Library
British and Irish Cinema and film periodicals at http://www.bl.uk/collections/cinema.html; and a select List of Victorian illustrated newspapers and journals at http://www.bl.uk/collections/victoria.html.

Film archives

The prospect of consulting a regional or national film archive can at first seem a very daunting and expensive prospect. Archives are becoming increasingly reactive to the needs of ordinary researchers and students. In many cases archives and collections provide online catalogues and resources. For a full list of UK regional film archives see the Film Archive Forum Website: www.bufvc.ac.uk/faf/faf.htm.

The Public Record Office
The PRO holds the official records of the country, generated by the government and the courts. It is a most important source for primary information about the commercial history of early film in the UK and film copyright. A comprehensive guide is available on microfiche, and this is updated on a regular basis. The PRO holdings are very extensive, and it is essential to prepare thoroughly before visiting, in order to avoid wasted time. Again you can search their PROCAT database on-line at http://www.cataloguespro.gov.uk/.

Museums and collections

An increasing number of museums and private collections are becoming accessible on-line. They provide varying types of historical and research materials but are often invaluable repositories of artefacts, films and ephemera, and should be consulted as a matter of course.

Bibliotheque Du Film (BIFI) Paris
http://www.bifi.fr

Bill Douglas Centre for the History of Cinema and Popular Culture
http://info.ex.ac.uk/billdouglas/mainmenu.html

British Film Institute
http://www.bfi.org.uk

National Fairground Archive
http://www.shef.ac.uk/uni/projects/nfa

National Museum of Photography, Film & Television
http://www.nmsi.ac.uk/nmpft

Organisations and on-line publications

Many on-line resources dedicated to the study of early cinema are now available, and offer commentaries, reviews, articles and historic documents. They are also an invaluable source of information regarding new discoveries, conferences and screenings.

Association Francaise De Recherche Sur L'Histoire Du Cinema
This site is available in an English version and contains a comprehensive series of useful links: http://www.soso.cnrs.fr/AFRHC/AFRHCE.html

Domitor
An association dedicated to the study of early cinema: http://cri.histart.unmontreal.ca/Domitor.

GRAFICS
Early cinema study group: http://cri.histart.unmontreal.ca/grafics/

The Magic Lantern Society
http://www.magiclantern.org.uk

The Projection Box
A publishing and information site which includes a virtual tour of the Museum of the Moving Image: http://easyweb.easynet.co.uk/~s-herbert/ProjectionBox.htm

Screening the Past
http://www.latrobe.edu.au/www/screeningthepast

On-line histories and sources

The Complete History of the Discovery of Cinematography
http://www.yesic.com/~fool/

Early cinema.com
http://earlycinema.com

Early Cinema Gateway
A major source of early cinema links: http://website.lineone.net/~lukemckernan/Links.htm

Film History, Studies and Education
http://www.rtvf.nwu.edu./links/studies.html

La Lanterna Magica (The Magic Lantern)
http://minicizotti.it

The Silent Film Bookshelf
Publishes essential documents relating to early cinema: http://cinemaweb.com/silentfilm/bookshelf

Silent Film Sources
http://www.cinemaweb.com/silentfilm/

Victoria Research Web
Scholarly resources for Victorian research: http://www.indianna.edu/~victoria/

Moving images on-line

The American Film Institute
http://www.afionline.org/home.html

The Early Cinema
This site contains several downloadable early films.
http://chmn.gmu.edu/courses/magic/movies/movieindex.html

Early Motion Pictures from The Library of Congress
An essential resource of on-line films between 1897–1916, with a comprehensive catalogue and information: http://lcweb2.loc.gov/papr/mpixhome.html

Pioneers and companies

The American Mutoscope and Biograph Co, Inc., USA.
http://www.muto1895.com

British Pathé Database
http://www.britishpathe.com/search.html

Thomas A. Edison Papers
http://edison.rutgers.edu/

King of the Movies: Siegfried Lubin
http://www.mc3.edu/gen/faculty/jeckhard/lubin.htm

George Méliès
http://www.alphacentauri.be/friends/Melies

The Mitchell and Kenyon Collection
http://www.bfi.org.uk/collections/mk/index.html

Tanhouser Film Co. (1909–17)
http://www.teleport.com/~tco

Charles Urban
http://website.lineone.net/~luke.mckernan/Urban.htm

Alfred West F.R.G.S.- Film Pioneer
http://mcs.open.ac.uk/dac3/ournavy/

Current journals

A number of journals are dedicated to studies in and related to early cinema; they provide an essential source of current academic approaches to the field and will enable students to keep abreast of new cutting edge material.

Film History
Griffithiana
Journal of Popular British Cinema
Kintop
Living Pictures: The Journal of the Popular and Projected Image before 1914
The Magic Lantern Journal
Picture House
Journal of Theatre Studies
Velvet Light Trap
Viewfinder
Wide Angle

Films sources

An essential part of the process of studying early cinema is the viewing of film itself. It can be very frustrating to constantly read about specific films without ever having the opportunity to view them. Whilst the situation is rapidly improving due to the development of digital technologies, the availability of films is still relatively poor. You should take any opportunity to view films seriously, and take advantage of a number of video/DVD resources which are commercially available. The on-line resources already highlighted provide invaluable supplementary material, but do not approach the experience of viewing films on the cinema screen. Prints are available for hire from the British Film Institute, they can be viewed either at their Stephen Street facilities, or through regional film archives. Many regional film theatres offer silent film events and you should also attempt to attend as many as possible. There are also a number of national and international conferences catering for early cinema. Attendance can seem a daunting prospect for students, but most offer reduced fees and they are a stimulating and supportive environment in which to see films and discuss ideas.

Video
Early Cinema: Primitives and Pioneers Vol 1 (BFI)
Early Cinema: Primitives and Pioneers Vol 2 (BFI)
Early Russian Cinema Vols 1–10 (BFI)

DVD
The Movies Begin- A Treasury of Early Cinema 1894–1913 (Kino Video-5 DVD set)

Conferences/events

The British Silent Cinema Weekend, The Broadway Cinema Nottingham
http://www.broadway.org.uk/home/silent.html

The Pordenone Silent Film Festival, Sacile Italy
http://www.cinetecadelfriuli.org/gcm/

GLOSSARY

cinema/early cinema
In this book, 'cinema' refers especially to the overall collection of institutions and cultures associated with film. The term is most easily understood in the post-1908 period in the US and UK, when the construction of static buildings solely dedicated to film exhibition – which we today call 'cinemas' – began a process of consolidation within the film industry. In this context, a coherent conception of the cinema is relatively easy to 'pin down'. However, the looser association of institutions and cultures of earlier film may equally be referred to as an 'early cinema' provided the term is used to refer inclusively to this loose association.

cinema of attractions
Developed from the theoretical work of Sergei Eisenstein by Tom Gunning and André Gaudreault in the context of early film studies, this term refers to a cinema dependent on shock, spectacle and the active collaboration of audiences. As such it is frequently opposed to the classical cinema, which depends upon the passive response of audiences to the more sedate pleasures afforded by fictional narrative.

classical cinema
The form and style of classical cinema is exemplified by Hollywood film production of the 1930s and 1940s. This was a narrative-driven fictional cinema in which the film's chain of events was motivated by the actions of characters. Classical cinema favours closed endings, and generally does not encourage its audiences to ask questions that might disrupt the film's self-enclosed fictional world.

early film
In this book, 'early film' refers to the medium of film and to its related social, cultural, and economic influences and consequences in the period 1895–1914.

institution
An institution can be described as an organisation, often associated with a particular infra-structure, with the capacity to persist through long periods of time and to influence a large number of people. In early film studies, institutional research concentrates on the role played by institutions such as film production companies and exhibition sites in the marketing, distribution, and reception of films.

mise-en-scène
A term derived from the French theatre literally meaning 'putting into a scene' and referring to the meaningful arrangement of space on-screen.

pre-cinema
A controversial and increasingly rejected term used to describe a range of technologies such as optical toys and magic lanterns which pre-date the arrival of commercial cinema. The use of this term is discouraged as it assumes that cinema is the result of a linear, technologically determined progression from one technology to another. The term has also distorted the historical study of these independent forms and has, in extreme cases, fixed their context as wholly one which presages the advent of cinema.

Primitive Mode of Representation (PMR)
According to Noël Burch, the PMR in early film refers to such features as the dominance of single-shot movies, the prevalence of films without narrative closure, and to the active collaboration of audiences and exhibitors typified by the presence of a lecturer. These ideas were also reflected in the later development of the cinema of attractions model, but this model also justifiably criticised the supposed 'primitivity' of the PMR, which neglected to specify the remarkable sophistication of early exhibition strategies.

BIBLIOGRAPHY

Essential reading

Chanan, M. (1996) *The Dream That Kicks: The Prehistory and Early Years of Cinema in Britain*. London: Routledge.

Christie, I. (1995) *The Last Machine: Early Cinema and the Birth of the Modern World*. London: BFI.

Cherchi Usai, P. (2000) *Silent Cinema: An Introduction*. London: BFI.

Elsaesser, T. with A. Barker (eds) (1990) *Early Cinema: Space, Frame, Narrative*. London: BFI.

Fullerton, J. (ed.) (1998) *Celebrating 1895: The Centenary of Cinema*. Sydney: John Libby.

Herbert, S. and L. McKernan (eds) (1996) *A Who's Who of Victorian Cinema: A Worldwide Survey*. London: BFI.

Higson, A. (2002) *Young and Innocent?: The Cinema in Britain 1896–1930*. Exeter: Exeter University Press.

Musser, C. (1994) *The Emergence of Cinema: The American Screen to 1907*. Berkeley and Los Angeles: University of California Press.

Rossell, D. (1998) *Living Pictures: The Origins of the Movies*. Albany, NY: State University of New York Press.

Tsivian, Y. (1998) *Early Cinema in Russia and its Cultural Reception*. Chicago and London: University of Chicago Press.

Williams, C. (ed.) (1996) *Cinema: the Beginnings and the Future: Essays Marking the Centenary of the first Film Show Projected to a Paying Audience in Britain*. London: University of Westminster Press.

Secondary reading

Abel, R. (ed.) (1996) *Silent Film*. New Brunswick, NJ: Rutgers University Press.
___ (1998) *The Ciné Goes to Town: French Cinema 1896–1914*. Berkeley and Los Angeles: University of California Press.
___ (1999) *The Red Rooster Scare: Making Cinema American 1900–1910*. Berkeley and Los Angeles: University of California Press.
Abel, R. and R. Altman (eds) (2001) *The Sounds of Early Cinema*. Bloomington: Indiana University Press.
Allen, R. C. and D. Gomery (1985) *Film History. Theory and Practice*. New York and London: McGraw Hill Publishing.
Anon. (1896a) *St. Paul's Magazine,* 7 March.
Anon. (1896b) 'An interview with Robert William Paul', *The Era*, 25 April.
Anon. (1897) 'How Dealers Make Money Out of Kinematographs', *The Photographic Dealer*, August.
Anon. (1899) 'The Cinematograph in Surgery', *Chambers's Journal*, 26 August.
Anon. (1900a) *The Optical Magic Lantern Journal*, March, 3.
Anon. (1900b) *The Photogram*, July, 300.
Anon. (1906) 'Army Cinematographs', *The Field Officer*, October.
Anon. (1908) 'Film-Picture Actors', *The Bioscope*, 2 October, 18.
Anon. (1909a) 'Tell-Tale Photograph: Wife's deception at a Cinematograph Show', *The World's Fair*, 2 October.
Anon. (1909b) 'Big Game Hunting by Cinematograph: How to Bag a Rhinoceros in the Parlour', *The World's Fair*, 3 July.
Anon. (1909c) 'The Making of a Picture. No. 1.', *The Rinking World and Picture Theatre News*, 4 December, 21.
Anon. (1911a) *Walturdaw Company Limited Catalogue*, 215.
Anon. (1911b) 'Plots for Picture Plays: Concocting Thrilling Dramas and Farcical Fakes for the Cinematograph', *The World's Fair*, 24 June, 11.
Anon. (1911c) *How to Run a Picture Theatre*. London: The Kinematograph Weekly.
Anon. (1913a) 'Judge On Picture Shows', *The Times*, 25 October.
Anon. (1913b) 'Training of Omnibus Drivers: The Cinematograph and the prevention of accidents', *The Times,* 2 May.
Anon. (1913c) 'The Cinematograph in Education: A Striking Experiment', *The Times*, 27 October.
Anon. (1914) 'The Cinema and the Young: Boys Bound Over Not to Enter Picture Theatres', *The Times*, 13 February.
Anon. (1917) *The Cinema, Its Present Position and Future Possibilities. Being the report of and chief evidence taken at the Cinema Commission of Enquiry.* London: Williams and Norgate.
Anthony, B. (1996) *The Kinora: Motion Pictures for the Home 1896–1914*. London: The Projection Box.
Bailey, P. (ed.) (1986) *Music Hall: The Business of Pleasure*. Milton Keynes: Open University Press.
Ball, E. H. (1913) *The Art of the Photoplay*: New York: Veritas.
Bazin, A. (1967) *What is Cinema?*, trans. Hugh Gray: Berkeley: University of

California.

Barnes, J. (1996a) *The Beginnings of Cinema in England: Volume 2, 1897*. Exeter: Exeter University Press.

____ (1996b) *The Beginnings of Cinema in England: Volume 3, 1898*. Exeter: Exeter University Press.

____ (1996c) *The Beginnings of Cinema in England: Volume 4, 1899*. Exeter: Exeter University Press.

____ (1997) *The Beginnings of Cinema in England: Volume 5, 1900*. Exeter: Exeter University Press.

____ (1998) *The Beginnings of Cinema in England: Volume 1, 1894–1896*. Exeter: Exeter University Press.

Bottomore, S. (1980) 'Frederick Villiers: War Correspondent', *Sight and Sound*, 49, 4, 250–5.

____ (1984) 'Dreyfus and Documentary', *Sight and Sound*, 53, 290–3.

____ (1995a) *I Want to See this Annie Mattygraph: A Cartoon History of the Coming of the Movies*. Pordenone: Le Giornate del Cinema Muto.

____ (ed.) (1998a) 'Cinema Pioneers', *Film History*, 10, 1.

____ (1998b) '"She's just Like my Granny! Where's Her Crown?" Monarchs and Movies, 1896–1916', in J. Fullerton (ed.) *Celebrating 1895: The Centenary of Cinema*. Sydney: John Libby, 172–81.

Bowser, E. (1994) *The Transformation of Cinema: 1907–1915*. Berkeley and Los Angeles: University of California Press.

Braun, M. (1992) *Picturing Time: The Work of Etienne-Jules Marey*. Chicago: University of Chicago Press.

Brown, R. and B. Anthony (1999) *A Victorian Film Enterprise: The History of the British Mutoscope and Biograph Company*. Trowbrdge: Flicks Books.

Burch, N. (1990) *Life to Those Shadows*, trans. and ed. B. Brewster. London: BFI.

Burton, A. and L. Porter (eds) (2000) *Pimple, Pranks and Pratfalls: British Film Comedy Before 1930*. Trowbridge: Flicks Books.

____ (eds) (2001) *The Showman, the Spectacle and the Two-Minute Silence: Performing British Cinema before 1930*. Trowbridge: Flicks Books.

____ (eds) (2002) *Crossing the Pond: Anglo-American Film Relations Before 1930*. Trowbridge: Flicks Books.

Calvert, C. (1917) 'Foreword', in W. J. Elliot, *How to Become a Film Actor*. London: The Picture Palace News Co., 4.

Crangle, R. (1998) 'Saturday Night at the X-Rays – The Moving Picture and "New Photography" in Britain, 1896', in J. Fullerton (ed.) *Celebrating 1895: The Centenary of Cinema*. Sydney: John Libby, 138–44.

Crarey, J. (2001) Suspensions of Perception: Attention, Spectacle, and Modern Culture. Cambridge, Massachusetts: MIT Press.

de Cordova, R. (1990) *Picture Personalities: The Emergence of the Star System in America*. Chicago: University of Illinois.

Delsarte, F. (1887) 'Delsarte's Own Words', in *Delsarte System of Oratory: Including the Complete Work of M. L'Abbe Delamosne and Mme. Angelique Arnaud (Pupils of Delsarte) with the Literary Remains of François Delsarte*. New York: Edgar S. Werner, 466.

Dixon, B. and L. McKernan (eds) (1999) British Silent Comedy Films: Viewing Copies in the National Film and Television Archive. London: BFI.

Eisenstein, S. M. (1988) 'The Montage of Film Attractions', in R. Taylor (ed.) Selected Works, 3 vols. London: BFI, I, 39–58.

Elsaesser, T. (1981) 'Narrative Cinema and Audience-Oriented Aesthetics', in T. Bennett et al. (eds) Popular Television and Film. Milton Keynes: Open University Press, 270–82.

Esenswein, J. B. and A. Leeds (1913) Writing the Photoplay. Springfield, Massachusetts: Home Correspondence School.

Fell, J. (ed.) (1983) Film Before Griffith. Berkeley and Los Angeles: University of California Press.

Fitzsimmons, L. and S. Street (eds) (2000) Moving Performance: British Stage and Screen, 1890s–1920s. Trowbridge: Flicks Books.

Fletcher, T. (2001 a) 'The London County Council and The Cinematograph, 1896–1900', Living Pictures: The Journal of The Popular and Projected Image before 1914, 1, 2, 69–83.

Garcia, G. (1882) The Actor's Art: A Practical Treatise on Stage Declamation, Public Speaking and Deportment. London: T. Pettitt, 113–66.

Gaudreault, A. (1990a) 'Showing and Telling: Image and Word in Early Cinema', in T. Elsaesser with A. Barker (eds) Early Cinema: Space, Frame, Narrative: London: BFI, 274–81.

____ (1990b) 'Film, Narrative, Narration: The Film of the Lumière Brothers', in T. Elsaesser with A. Barker (eds) Early Cinema: Space, Frame, Narrative. London: BFI, 68–75.

____ (1990c) 'The Infringement of Copyright Laws and its Effects', in T. Elsaesser with A. Barker (eds) Early Cinema: Space, Frame, Narrative. London: BFI, 114–22.

Gifford, D. (1987) Books and Plays in films, 1896–1915: Literary, Theatrical and Artistic Sources of the First Twenty Years of Motion Pictures. London and Jefferson, NC: Mansell.

____ (2001a) The British Film Catalogue, Vol.1: The Fiction Film, 1895–1994. London: Fitzroy Dearborn.

____ (2001b) The British Film Catalogue, Vol.2: The Non-Fiction Film, 1895–1994. London: Fitzroy Dearborn.

Gorky, M. (1896) Nizhegorodski listok, in C.Harding and S. Popple (eds) [1996] In The Kingdom of Shadows: a Companion to Early Cinema. London: Cygnus Arts Press, 5.

Gray, F. (ed.) (1996) The Hove Pioneers and the Arrival of Cinema. Brighton: University of Brighton.

____ (2002) 'James Williamson's Rescue Narratives', in A. Higson (ed.) Young and Innocent?: The Cinema in Britain 1896–1930. Exeter: Exeter University Press, 28–41.

Gunning, T. (1986) 'The Cinema of Attractions: Early Film, Its Spectator and the Avant-Garde', Wide Angle, 8, 3/4, 63–70.

____ (1989) 'An Aesthetic of Astonishment: Early Film and the (In)credulous Spectator', Art and Text, 34, 31–45.

____ (1991) *D. W. Griffith and the Origins of American Narrative Film: The Early Years at Biograph*. Chicago, IL: University of Illinois.

____ (1997) 'In Your Face: Physiognomy, Photography, and the Gnostic Mission of Early Film', *MODERNISM/modernity*, 4, 1–29.

Harding, C. and S. Popple (eds) (1996) *In The Kingdom of Shadows: a Companion to Early Cinema*. London: Cygnus Arts Press.

Heard, M. (2000) '"Come in Please, Come Out Pleased": The development of British Fairground Bioscope Presentation and Performance', in L. Fitzsimmons and S. Street (eds) *Moving Performance: British Stage and Screen, 1890s–1920s*. Trowbridge: Flicks Books, 101–11.

Hecht, A. (1993) *Pre-Cinema History: An Encyclopaedia and Annotated Bibliography of the Moving Image before 1896*. London: Bowker-Saur/BFI.

Hepworth, C. (1896) 'On the Lantern Screen', *The Amateur* Photographer, 6 November.

Hepworth, C. (1951) *Came the Dawn: Memoirs of a Film Pioneer*. London: Phoenix House.

Herbert, S., C. Harding and S. Popple (eds) (1996) *Victorian Film Catalogues: A Facsimile Collection*. London: The Projection Box.

Herbert, S. (ed.) (2000) *A History of Early Film*. London: Routledge.

Hiley, N. (1998) ' At the Picture Palace: The British Cinema Audience, 1895–1920', in J. Fullerton (ed.) *Celebrating 1895: The Centenary of Cinema*. Sydney: John Libby, 96–103.

____ (2000) '"No mixed bathing": the creation of the British Board of Film Censors in 1913', *Journal of Popular British Cinema*, 3, 200, 5–19.

____ (2002) 'Nothing More than a "Craze": Cinema Building in Britain from 1909-1914', in A. Higson (ed.) *Young and Innocent?: The Cinema in Britain 1896–1930*. Exeter: Exeter University Press, 111–17.

Hopwood, H. (1899) *Living Pictures, Their History, Photo-Production, and Practical Working*. London. Optician and Photographic Trades Review.

Hulfish, D. S. (1915) *Motion Picture Work: A General Treatise on PictureTaking, Picture Making, Photo-Plays, and Theater Management and Operation*. Chicago: American Technical Society.

Jenkins, C. (1898) 'Animated Pictures', *The Photographic Times*, 7 July.

Johnson, V. E. (1896) 'The Kinematograph from a Scientific Point of View', *Photography*, 10 December.

Kember, J. (2000) '"It was not the show, it was the tale that you told": film lecturing and showmanship on the British fairground', in S. Popple and V. Toulmin (eds) *Visual Delights: Essays on the Popular and Projected Image in the 19^(th) Century*. Trowbridge: Flicks Books, 61–70.

____ (2001) 'Face to Face: The Facial Expressions Genre in Early British Film', in A. Burton and L. Porter (eds) *The Showman, the Spectacle and the Two-Minute Silence: Performing British Cinema before 1930*. Trowbridge: Flicks Books, 28–39.

____ (2003) 'The View from the Top of Mont Blanc: The Alpine Entertainment in Victorian Britain', *Living Pictures*, 3, forthcoming.

Kirton, J. W. (n.d.) *Buy Your Own Cherries*. London: Richard J. James & Son.

Liesegang, F. P. (1986) *Dates and Sources: A Contribution to the History of the Art of Projection and to Cinematography*. London: Magic Lantern Society.

Hopwood, H.(1899) *Living Pictures, Their History, Photo-Production, and Practical Working*. London. Optician and Photographic Trades Review.

Low, R. and R. Manvell (1997) *The History of the British Film, 1896–1906*. London: Routledge.

Mannoni, L., D. Presenti Campagnoni and D. Robinson (1995) *Light and Movement: Incunabula of the Motion Picture*. Pordenone: Le Giornate Del Cinema Muto.

McKernan, L. (1992) *Topical Budget: The Great British News Film*. London: BFI.

_____ (1996) 'Sport and the First Films', in C. Williams (ed.) *Cinema: the Beginnings and the Future: Essays Marking the Centenary of the first Film Show Projected to a Paying Audience in Britain*. London: University of Westminster Press, 107–16.

_____ (1999) *The Boer War: The Holdings of the National Film and Television Archive*. London: BFI.

_____ (2000) '"That slick salesman in the silk hat": Charles Urban arrives in Britain', in S. Popple and V. Toulmin (eds) *Visual Delights: Essays on the Popular and Projected Image in the 19th Century*. Trowbridge: Flicks Books, 116–26.

_____ (2002) 'Putting the World Before You: The Charles Urban Story', in A. Higson (ed.) *Young and Innocent?: The Cinema in Britain 1896–1930*. Exeter: Exeter University Press, 65–77.

Medhurst, A. (1986) 'Music Hall and British Cinema', in C. Barr (ed.) *All our Yesterdays: 90 Years of British Cinema*. London: BFI, 168–88.

Montgomery, H. B. (1913) *How to Form, Conduct, and Manage a Picture Theatre Company*. London: Kinematograph and Lantern Weekly Ltd.

Musser, C. (1979) 'The Early Cinema of Edwin Porter', *Cinema Journal*, 29, 1.

Musser, C. and C. Nelson (1991) *Lyman H. Howe and the Forgotten Era of Travelling Exhibition 1880–1920*: Princeton: Princeton University Press.

Norman, T. (n.d.) *Memoirs of Tom Norman: The Silver King*. Sheffield University Library: National Fairground Archive.

Pearson, G. (1938) 'Lambeth Walk to Leicester Square', *Sight and Sound*, 7, 28, 150.

Pearson, R. (1992) *Eloquent Gestures: The Transformation of Performance Styles in the Griffith Biograph Films*. Berkeley: University of California.

Popple, S. (1996) 'The Diffuse Beam: Cinema and Change', in C. Williams (ed.) *Cinema: the Beginnings and the Future: Essays Marking the Centenary of the first Film Show Projected to a Paying Audience in Britain*. London: University of Westminster Press, 97–106.

_____ (1998) '"Cinema Wasn't Invented, It Growed": Technological Film Historiography Before 1913', in J. Fullerton (ed.) *Celebrating 1895: The Centenary of Cinema*. Sydney: John Libby, 19–26.

_____ (2002) '"But the Khaki-Covered Camera is the *Latest* Thing": The Boer War Cinema and Visual Culture in Britain', in A. Higson (ed.) *Young and Innocent?: The Cinema in Britain 1896–1930*. Exeter: Exeter University Press, 13–27.

Popple, S. and V. Toulmin (eds) (2000) *Visual Delights: Essays on the Popular and Projected Image in the 19th Century*. Trowbridge: Flicks Books.

Ricketson, S. (1986) *The Berne Convention for the Protection of Literary and Artistic Works: 1886–1986*. London: Centre for Commercial Law Studies.

Robins, E. (1897) 'Hints on Exhibiting Cinematographs', *The Optical Magic Lantern Journal*, August.

Rossell, D. (1995) 'A Chronology of cinema, 1889–1896', *Film History*, 7, 2.

____ (2000) 'A Slippery job: travelling exhibitors in early cinema', in S. Popple and V. Toulmin (eds) *Visual Delights: Essays on the Popular and Projected Image in the 19th Century*. Trowbridge: Flicks Books, 50–60.

____ (1992) *Film Style and Technology: History and Analysis*. London: Starword Press.

Sopocy, M. (1996) 'The Role of the Intertitle in Film Exhibition, 1910–1914', in C. Williams (ed.) *Cinema: the Beginnings and the Future: Essays Marking the Centenary of the first Film Show Projected to a Paying Audience in Britain*. London: University of Westminster Press, 123–34.

Stewart, H. (ed.) (1996) *Early and Silent Cinema: A Source Book*. London: BFI.

Sturgess, A. and A. Collins (1899) *Theatre Royal, Drury Lane Grand Christmas Pantomime: Jack and the Beanstalk*. London: Nassau Press.

Tagg, J. (1988) *The Burden of Representation: Essays on Photographies and Histories*. London: Macmillan.

Talbot, F. A. (1912) *Moving Pictures: How they are made and worked*. London: William Heinemann.

Toulmin, V. (1994) 'Telling the Tale: The Story of the Fairground Bioscope Shows and the Showmen Who Operated Them', *Film History*, 6, 2, 219–37.

____ (1996a) 'The Fairground Bioscope', in C. Harding and S. Popple (eds) *In The Kingdom of Shadows: a Companion to Early Cinema*. London: Cygnus Arts Press, 191–3.

____ (1996b) 'Travelling Shows and the first Static Cinemas', *Picture House*, Summer, 5–12.

____ (1998a) *Randall Williams: King of the Showmen. From Ghost Show to Bioscope*. London: The Projection Box.

____ (2001) 'Local Films For Local People!: Travelling Showmen and the Commissioning of Local Films in Great Britain, 1900-1902', *Film History*, 13, 118–37.

Turvey, G. (2001) '*The Battle of Waterloo* (1913): The First British Epic', in A. Burton and L. Porter (eds) *The Showman, the Spectacle and the Two-Minute Silence: Performing British Cinema before 1930*. Trowbridge: Flicks Books, 40–7.

Whalley, R. and P. Warden (1998) 'Forgotten Firm: A Short Chronological Account of Mitchell and Kenyon, Cinematographers', *Film History*, 10, 1, 35–51.

Whitby, J.E. (1900) 'The Future of the Cinematograph', *Chambers's Journal*, 19 May.

Williams, D. R. (1997) 'The Cinematograph Act of 1909: An Introduction to the Impetus Behind the Legislation and Some Early Effects', *Film History*, 9, 4, 341–50.